ORDINARY PEOPLE
EXTRAORDINARY STORIES

HUMANS OF BOMBAY

· presents ·

ORDINARY PEOPLE EXTRAORDINARY STORIES

KARISHMA MEHTA

First published in India by
HarperCollins *Publishers* 2021
A-75, Sector 57, Noida, Uttar Pradesh 201301, India
www.harpercollins.co.in

2 4 6 8 10 9 7 5 3 1

P-ISBN: 978-93-9032-726-3
E-ISBN: 978-93-9032-727-0

The stories and the facts in this book are as narrated to the author by the individual interviewees, and the author has proper permission from the interviewees to publish the same.

Cover design: Shivam Maurya
Author photo: Ryan Martis

Typeset in 9.75/12 FreightText Book
by Twisha Mehta.

Printed and bound at
Thomson Press (India) Ltd

HarperCollinsIn

"To hell with happy endings,
you are here for the story."
—Beau Taplin

To stories; the ones we tell, the ones we become.

EDITOR'S NOTE

I was twenty-one when I founded Humans of Bombay and through these eight years, I've had what seems like multiple MBA courses simultaneously. But slicing through the myriad of business, finance, and the whole schbang, the one invaluable skill we have honed, is the art of storytelling. And that's how even our seemingly simple questions like, 'How are you feeling today?' opens up the floodgates of all kinds of emotions. What does that tell you about humans? Ultimately, we all want to be heard.

The more we listened, the more people opened up about their lives. I still remember my first shoot—I traipsed Mumbai's iconic Marine Drive, asking strangers to speak with me. Only one woman agreed; she was in her mid fifties and recently widowed.

We sat there, two strangers, with the city lights twinkling behind us, knowing that we'd connected far beyond the 'stranger' tag. At the end of it, she said, 'Thank you, it feels like a burden has been lifted off my chest.' We parted ways, but I knew I was onto something special. Ever since, the team at Humans of Bombay loves to envelop strangers in a warm hug, to walk shoulder to shoulder with the rebels with a cause, and to just ... listen. This mantra has allowed us to move beyond 'likes', and add value to lives in a way we never imagined—crowdfunding.

We have thus far raised over fifteen crores, paying for surgeries, the education of the lesser privileged, rehabilitating women in the sex trade and in one case, justice for a man who was wrongfully imprisoned for a bomb blast.

We told Ali Bhai's story and then asked our readers to contribute twenty-three lakhs for the twenty-three years he spent in jail. Overnight, we raised the entire amount. When we broke this to Ali Bhai, he said—'The world is not all that bad; the world is still kind.' And I believe that with all my heart. Through the pandemic, the wars, and the politics of greed ... there is still love and kindness. So today, I hope you choose just that—to be kind to a stranger, to give to those who need, to vehemently express your love, every chance you get.

And this is me, taking that chance. This book is my love letter to the people of India. It has shades of jugaad, humble roots, and building a sense of unrelenting brotherhood that binds us together. Listening to these stories have changed me in a way that nothing else has. So I invite you to walk with me through the dusty streets and colourful nooks of a country with 1.3 billion beating hearts ... one story at a time.

I LIVE A SIMPLE LIFE. I start my day by 8.30 a.m. and finish around 5 p.m. My children love Chinese food, so on special occasions we surprise them with it! I go home, spend time with my wife and children, and watch TV. On most days, when I collect the dabbas and find that there's leftover food, I ask the owners for permission to distribute it to street kids by the tracks. It's out of the way for me and I get home later than usual, but it's worth the extra effort. So that's what my life's about—my family, my work, and these small, sweet moments strung together.

BULLETPROOF BOSS

I WAS SIXTEEN WHEN I FELL IN LOVE. HE WAS WILLING TO WAIT FOR ME WHILE I CHASED MY DREAM OF BECOMING A POLICE OFFICER.

But back then, you couldn't simply date someone—you had to get married. My father pressured me to make a choice—him or the uniform. I chose love, and believe me, it's the best decision I've ever made. He pushed me to be more than just a home-maker, to do exactly what I wanted to do.

Life was blissful and I was truly happy. I was studying criminology, which allowed me to interact with the police. It was like a balm for my ego, because I had managed to dip my feet into both worlds; I was not only playing my part in maintaining law and order, but also becoming a mom.

I clearly remember, in January 1987, I was watching a parade on TV with my baby in my lap, when the 'all-women' march came on the screen. It was a stinging reminder of my forgotten dreams—I couldn't help but get emotional. Times had finally changed and women were now allowed in the paramilitary—I couldn't let this opportunity pass me by. With the support of my husband and my family, I decided to apply.

I went on to become the first and only woman that qualified from South India. One of the physical tests is still burned into my memory—I had already sprained my ankle before the final 100 meter race. I chose to run with the guys, and despite my injury, I ran the race of my life! I gained the respect of every single person on that field.

I was the first woman in the Special Protection Group. I've had the honour of serving seven Prime Ministers of our country. A part of my job description was to be ready to take a bullet to protect the Prime Minister, but I never feared for my life because I knew my husband would take care of our sons. He had taken on the role of raising them, while I was chasing my dreams.

We'd finally settled into our lives—work was good, the kids were doing well, but there was still one piece missing from the puzzle. One morning, my husband suddenly brought home a forty-day

old German Shepherd puppy! We'd never really discussed having a pet, especially a dog, since I was more of a cat lady. But soon enough, Sheeba became the daughter I never had, and by the time Scooby came into our lives, I became a hard-core dog lover.

Unfortunately, around this time, my husband began to get very sick. He went on a pilgrimage for a few days ... but never came back home to me. He passed away suddenly, and for the first time in my life, I was completely alone; left with two beautiful children. I only cried when I was alone with my puppies—I attempted to fill the void my husband had left behind. I voluntarily retired from the military, and took up a corporate job instead. Because Sheeba and Scooby were instrumental in my own healing, I decided to adopt more dogs—I wanted to do something for them. People began to pick up on the fact that I was willing to rescue and foster dogs, and started showing up at my door with strays—I couldn't bring myself to turn away any of them.

By the time my children brought me back to Delhi from Chennai, we had thirty-five dogs under our care. In fact, the only way my sons managed to get me to move, was moving the dogs first—they knew mom would follow her babies wherever they went.

Finding an appropriate home to house our dogs was not an easy task. After multiple rejections, we took up a property on rent from someone I knew from my days in the army.

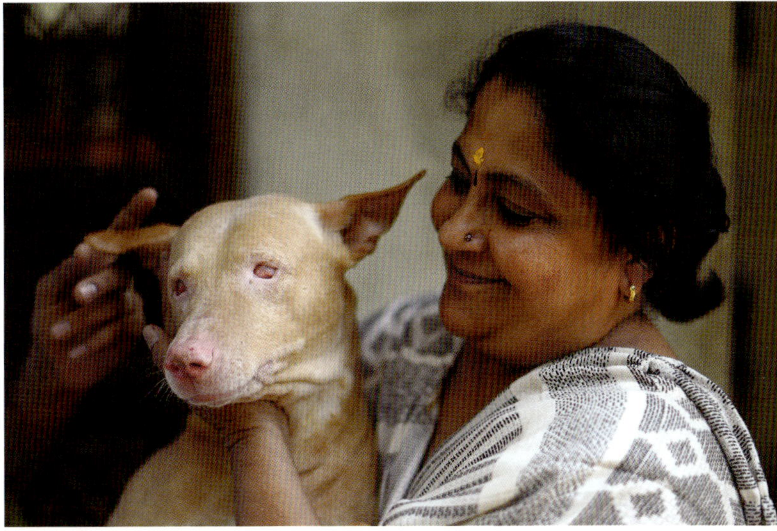

People just leave dogs they find on the streets at my home. In fact, the most recent addition was literally thrown over our gate just yesterday. We've actually run out of names for them now, and have resorted to giving them numbers—Alien 1 and Alien 2 are pretty much inseparable now.

Each and every abandoned dog that is placed in our home is first medically examined and then neutered. I have five employees and along with them we make over 300 rotis and 110 eggs every single day, and every dog is placed on a schedule for their baths. One of my sons stays with me, while my other son rescues his own dogs. Together, we take care of our family.

Unfortunately, we've made enemies out of our neighbours and quite often, the police come over and try to claim that we're running a breeding business. There is a lot of noise, and the space is beginning to become too small. The hospitals are too far away, and we lose so many of our dogs because there's no way to get them the medical attention they require. While neither my son nor I care about luxuries for ourselves, we cannot compromise on the quality of life we give them.

I'VE BEEN A PROTECTOR ALL MY LIFE.

So we've taken matters into our own hands. I've just sold my last property, and we've bought thirty-five thousand sq. ft of remote and open land that we'll be dedicating solely to our dogs. We'll have enough space to have an on-site medical team, a clinic, and anything else that could be required.

Some people think I'm crazy, but it really doesn't matter to me—they can say whatever they like. My dogs have helped me grieve, and now, I thank my husband every day for bringing Sheeba home. He, unintentionally, put me on this path. I only had twenty-two years with him ... and I couldn't save him. But what I can do, is save these dogs—from hunger, from cruelty, from death.

I've been a protector all my life—this is what I was born to do. It's almost second nature for me to aid in the protection of India, whether it be protecting our Prime Ministers, our citizens or these abandoned dogs. I've served this country all my life and I will continue to do so till my last breath.

I'M KNOWN AS THE 'HARE DARWAZE' WALE UNCLE—I've sold gems and precious stones in this spot since the past nineteen years. But the truth is, the things hara darwaza and I have seen together are the most precious—they are life lessons that only experience can give you. Like when twelve years ago, this older woman came here looking for a precious gem. It was taking me some time to find what she was looking for, so I said, 'Ek minute ruko, Didi.' At that point, she looked at me sternly and asked me to repeat what I'd said. I thought I'd offended her. I started apologising but she vehemently asked me to repeat myself. When I did, she started crying. In between sobs she told me that she'd suddenly lost her younger brother a year ago, and when I called her 'Didi', she saw him in me.

Ever since then, she calls me her brother and ties a Rakhi on my arm every year. She's from a wealthy family; I'm a stall owner. She's from a different part of the world; I'm from Jaipur. She's Hindu; I'm Muslim. This is one incident, but what I've realised by meeting people from all walks of life is that there's love and acceptance all around us, but we're torn apart by those who benefit from hate. Why else would the boys from the surrounding shops manage my stall when I have to go read my Namaz during Ramadan? Why would some of them ask me to inaugurate their shops out of respect for my experience and age? Why would I shower them with sweets and celebrate Diwali with them? Nineteen years and every raw experience from my street stall has taught me that we have the power to decide whether we're on the side of love, or on the side of hate ... And that choice is only yours—why would you choose anything else?

THE DAY GAURI WAS BORN AND I HELD HER FOR THE FIRST TIME, I knew I would move mountains for her. But when Gauri was four, I found out that my wife was having an affair. We'd been married for seven years, and had a beautiful daughter. I didn't want to believe it ... I even decided to give our marriage a second chance. But my wife said she was in love. I was hurt. But that's life, it happens. So, after trying for two years, we got divorced and my wife got Gauri's custody.

I was distraught, but I didn't want to challenge the court's decision—I didn't want my daughter to spend her weekends attending one hearing after another. So I made my peace seeing her every weekend. We developed a routine—every Saturday I would take her to eat burgers and donuts. But dropping her back after a blissful weekend was hard; the days that followed were harder. Sometimes she would call me at night, trying hard not to cry as she'd say, 'I miss you, Papa.' I knew she wanted to stay with me. She'd tell me she was planning on escaping but I'd just console her. On her eighth birthday, she refused to cut the cake without me. I had sworn to never enter my ex-wife's house, but when I heard her crying on her birthday, I forgot about everything else. That day, I told everyone I was going to bring her back home. Thankfully, my wife agreed; I gave them a year to make the transition. We celebrated Gauri's 9th birthday together.

It was Mother's Day a week after that and she made me a card that read, 'Happy Mother's Day, Papa.' That day, we both cried. We've both settled in well. Now, we do everything together, from watching movies to making stupid videos. I tend to her like a mother, fight with her like a sibling and care for her like a father. In return, she's my best friend; she carefully listens to everything I say and like any best friend, she tries to be my wing woman—'Get married now, Papa. I want to dance in your baraat!'

I TOLD MYSELF THAT ONE DAY, I'LL DO SOMETHING THAT CHANGES THE WAY THE WORLD LOOKS AT PLUS SIZED WOMEN.

IN SCHOOL I WAS CALLED NAMES LIKE 'MOTI', and I had teachers who used to make the 'fat girls' stay back and run around the playground. They wanted us to be embarrassed, so that we'd think twice before 'enjoying' our food. This didn't stop in college. I was studying fashion designing, and every designer had to model their own clothes. I was the only one who was assigned another 'thin' model. While my classmates flaunted their clothes, I had to sit in the shadows and watch someone else do that for me.

That was my tipping point. I realised I'd had enough of the shaming. I told myself that one day, I'll do something that changes the way the world looks at plus sized women. I started a blog, where I dressed up and posted photos, with captions on body positivity. One of my photos even went viral!

I continued to blog about my journey, to help people realise that beauty comes in all shapes and sizes. Soon, I received an offer to be the face of a brand, and even had a huge poster of myself inside a mall. I felt so proud.

Today, everything I've done, and the stage I'm at, is not to show my bullies that I'm better than them. It's to show the girl who's being mocked in school, or the woman who's being asked to lose weight at home, or the people who don't like what they see in the mirror, that they're beautiful just as they are. I want to tell them, 'You're you, and you're pretty amazing ... don't ever let anyone bring you down!

FIVE YEARS AGO, on my father's birthday, I went to an orphanage to distribute sweets ... that's when I saw Avnish for the first time. He was five months old. No one was paying any attention to him as he lay in a corner. I couldn't help myself. I went and picked him up. He laughed, and we just clicked. I asked the warden what was going to happen to these kids, and he told me that all but Avnish would get adopted. He said that Avnish was 'Paagal', had Down syndrome and was going to die in a few years anyway.

At home that night, I couldn't stop thinking about him ... about how he'd be alone the whole night, and how he had been just left to die. I went back to the orphanage and asked if they'd let me adopt Avnish.

They laughed and said that as a bachelor who was not even thirty years old yet, I couldn't adopt. I didn't know what to do, but I knew I couldn't give up. I started visiting the orphanage and spending time with Avnish. I even started asking about his medical condition and documentation to make sure he was being treated right. But every time I asked questions, the warden was dodgy. They eventually shifted Avnish to an orphanage in Bhopal, because they were tired of me snooping. I didn't relent—I wanted to be there for Avnish.

I drove down every weekend to meet him and even researched adoption laws in India. Everyday I'd write letters to ministers and public figures for help. I even got in touch with the child welfare council, but they said that they didn't have any record of Avnish.

That didn't sit well with me. I realised that there were many more undocumented kids at the orphanage and a lot of them were disappearing. I suspected they were victims of child and organ trafficking. I began to file petitions to bring the truth out and started getting calls from people, telling me to 'stay out' of the matter or something would happen to me.

Finally my breakthrough came when the Welfare Minister responded and said that she'd help me. That expedited everything, and soon that orphanage was exposed and banned.

After eleven months, I was finally given Avnish's custody, and the other kids were sent to a better home. It was the happiest moment of my life. I baby-proofed my house, spent nights understanding how to change diapers and how to take care of Down Syndrome babies.

The day Avnish came home, it was like sunshine walked into my life. I wouldn't be spending another night worrying about him, because he was right next to me. Today, it's been a few years and now Avnish even goes to play school! He calls me both mumma and papa, because mostly he sees moms coming to pick their kids up at school.

When I go to work, he stays at daycare and at night we play and read.

He's the best thing that's happened to me, he's my world, he's my son and together, we're going to make this life a special one.

AND THE DAY AVNISH CAME HOME,
IT WAS LIKE SUNSHINE WALKED INTO MY LIFE.

MY WIFE PASSED AWAY when my daughters were quite young, so I raised them on my own. And the happiest day of my life was when both of them got married and settled in their new homes. I decided to write off all my property in their name—just to make sure that they would always be secure. Little did I know that they would kick me out of their lives, and out of my own house. I'm sixty-two-years old and I've been sleeping in this park for eight years. I don't have a single penny to my name and I'm too weak to even get a job—I eat food at the nearby temples. I honestly don't even remember the last time I spoke to my daughters, but, if I ever do talk to them, I won't ask them to give me back what's mine—they can keep it. I don't care about any of that. I'm alive and I'm surviving—and one day I know I'll somehow build a new life for myself... I'll find a home for myself. And that hope is what keeps me going.

PEOPLE THINK OF ME AS AN ORDINARY KULFIWAALA. And maybe they are right, but I'll let you decide. I started off with my tan-tan cart at the age of nine. I'd alternate between the streets of Civil Lines and Mansarovar. But once, while resting near Sawai Man Singh Hospital, Maharani Gayatri Devi walked down the stairs of the hospital and stopped in front of my cart ... it was peak summer and she wanted to have kulfi!

'Oh wow! Khoob kamayi hui hogi!'

Are you crazy? How stupid would I be to take money from the most beautiful woman in the world?!

'Achha, anyone else?'

Yes, of course! In the sixty-one years of running this business I have served Govinda, Shashi Kapoor Ji and even Hema Malini Ji. I am sure if you ask them of their time in Jaipur, they will tell you about the amazing kulfi they had.

THEY SAY THAT, the strength of motherhood is greater than the natural laws, and this was proved when I was carrying my second son Balaji. I was diagnosed with Meningitis during my second month of pregnancy. Initially, we didn't know what it was. I slowly started experiencing memory loss and eventually I couldn't even recognise people. The condition worsened with every passing day and I was unconscious and hospitalised until my eighth month of pregnancy.

I don't remember what happened through the months but I clearly remember 14 November 1989. That was the day I had held my bundle of joy in my arms. I felt like I had entered into the world of a whole new perspective! All the pain, suffering and everything else just disappeared; all I could see was my son, my baby and his brightest eyes that had brought so much happiness in my life.

THE WORLD WILL JUDGE YOU NO MATTER WHAT, SO LIVE THE LIFE THE WAY YOU WANT.

In April 2018, my elder son sent me a video of TedX talk by Balaji, and it was then that I discovered that my son was gay. I was surprised and overwhelmed. A lot of things were going on in my mind, I felt really bad that he had to fight so many battles all alone and I couldn't do anything for him. I also felt proud of my baby, who had grown up enough to accept and embrace who he was. I watched the video over and over again and then finally decided to call him. I couldn't even talk to him.

I literally broke into tears the moment I heard his voice. I just told him one thing, 'The world will judge you no matter what, so live your life the way you want to. No matter what happens, remember that I will always be there by your side'. Since then, with every passing day, I've been increasingly proud of how he inspires so many people to come out of the closet.

There have been times when I have had a lot of people, including my own relatives, talking ill about him. All I tell them is that every individual has a right to live their life with their own identity and we are nobody to judge them for who they are. I remember the director of my school asking me, 'Aren't you embarrassed by the way your son dresses?' I just told him, 'that is how he likes to dress and it gives him happiness. He prefers wearing a ghagra over pants and I don't think that is something I must be embarrassed of, instead I am proud of the fact that he lives his life fearlessly accepting himself for who he is!' I know there are still so many parents out there who haven't accepted their kids who have come out of the closet, and there are kids who are scared to be rejected by their parents.

All I would like to tell them is no matter who they choose to be, at the end of the day they need their parents the most, especially when society around them is so judgemental. We have to support them for who they are, it doesn't matter if your son prefers pink or your daughter likes to play with cars instead of Barbie dolls, if that gives them happiness, then be it! Let them live their lives beyond stereotypes and be proud of whoever they are!

“ SOME DAYS WE GET A SLIGHT SMILE FROM HER OR A NOD AND WE KNOW THAT'S SHE'S LISTENING.

I **STILL REMEMBER THE DAY** like it was yesterday. I was so excited to be home for Diwali and see my parents. Mom came to pick me up and on the way back we stopped at a cafe for a quick bite.

We were going up the stairs—she was walking slowly and I was excitedly running up, when I heard a loud thud. I turned around and I saw that mom had slipped. She was lying in a pool of blood, with her right ear bleeding and her skull completely fractured.

I was trembling with shock. I called my dad and tried to tell him what had happened. People had gathered, but none of them were helping. I was only thirteen. Some men started to touch me and my mom inappropriately. I didn't know what to do. Thankfully, one man came, wrapped napkins around mom's head and took us to the hospital. She was in critical care for a few days, until she slipped into a coma. I was heartbroken. I kept thinking that it was my fault—my fault that I didn't walk with her; that I couldn't get her to the hospital in time and that I may not be able to talk to her ever again. She's my best friend. I remember we used to go out for drives so often, just her and I. I'd play all the latest pop songs and dance and she'd try to imitate me and pretend to like the songs just for me. We've tried everything—consulting doctors, trying different therapies ... but nothing's worked. One doctor even went to the extent of telling us that there's no point in keeping her alive.

That was when my dad said to me, 'If Lavita was in my place, she would never let either of us go. If you're with me, we will fight this together.' So we got her home. We got nurses to care for her. Each day we try to help her heal—my dad and I talk to her, help her exercise and reminisce about happier times. Some days we get a slight smile from her or a nod and we know that's she's listening.

I think of all the times she took an off from work without thinking, to take care of me when I was sick, or how if I was ever upset and didn't want to talk, she'd just get me a big bowl of my favourite ice-cream. I think of those things and know that there's no way I'm giving up on her—I know that one day we'll be the perfect family again. The three of us, with mom laughing and being our biggest strength ... the way she always has been.

MY CHILDHOOD was mostly about coming to terms with my sexuality. I would try out mom's saris when she wasn't at home, and liked playing 'house' with girls rather than cricket with the boys. I was fascinated with my sister's clothes and was often bullied by my classmates and called 'chakka' or 'baila'.

When I tried to 'fit in' and play hide-and-seek with the boys in my building, they would ask me to touch their private parts. It was the same story with the boys at school—they would corner me and ask me to measure their penises. When I reached out to my family for help, I was shunned. I was told to mend my ways and start 'acting like a boy'.

My tipping point was when my teacher came and asked me whether I was a boy or a girl. I was shocked—not by the question, but by the person who had asked me the question. I'd had enough.

In 2015, I wore the most colourful sari I could find and went to the Mumbai Pride Parade. What a feeling that was—being myself, strangers coming up to me and appreciating my sari. Then the best thing happened! Vishal Srivastava, who was shooting for 'Wajood', met me there and offered me a role in his film.

MY NAME IS GANGA, I'M TRANSGENDER AND I'M CO-HOSTING A DANCE REALITY SHOW ON TV!

I couldn't believe my ears! That was the turning point in my life. The film was appreciated all over the world and people started to recognise me. People often associate transgenders with prostitution or begging, but I'd like to tell you this: My name is Ganga, I'm transgender and I'm co-hosting a dance reality show on TV! I've had some tough days, but I fought them all to finally find beauty in just being me. I stand tall and filled with pride to tell you all that the tough days may make you feel like it's the end sometimes, but it's actually just that nudge from the Universe to break free and take the leap of faith. Make the jump—trust me, you will fly!

SHE HIT ME YESTERDAY WHILE WE WERE PLAYING BUT I FORGAVE HER. IT'S OKAY, I STILL LOVE HER BECAUSE SHE'S MY YOUNGER SISTER.

YOU'RE LUCKY I'M IN A GOOD MOOD today, since I don't generally talk to people, especially strangers! My son called me an hour back and gave me the best news—bahu just delivered a baby boy! Main dadi maa ban gayi hun! But if I go there, who will sell these vegetables? Paise toh ab bhi kamane hain, and everyone from my family is already there. I don't want to crowd the place. In the evening, I will distribute motichoor ke ladoo in my colony but for now, I'm giving free ginger with every order. Roz roz thodi na dadi banta hai koi!

CHABBIS GYARA

9.20 P.M., CST I was setting up my stall when I heard a gunshot. When I got out to check, I saw a police officer telling other passengers to run.

The guy in the stall next to me said that people are firing—I froze. After that I saw a mother and her baby being shot—I went numb. Then they shot at my door and a bullet pierced my shoulder! I laid still on the floor. After twenty-seven minutes, the firing stopped and I got out. There were bodies everywhere, a few injured people were bleeding; I helped take them to the hospital. But I lost three friends—the man who ran a bookstore, the jhadu wala and the TC chacha. But I still come back here to work—I've kept the bullet marks inside my stall to remember. The fear is still there, but so is the regret. Kasab and Ismail were five feet away from me—if I had a pistol I could have shot them and ended it right there. But their carnage had just begun.

9.40 P.M., LEOPOLD CAFE I was on night duty at Colaba Wadi that night. Around 9.20 we got a message on the wireless that there's some 'gadbad' happening at Leopold. My initial hunch was that it had to do with the fact that there was an India-England cricket match that night. We'd won, so I thought people were bursting crackers and creating some ruckus. So four of us cops made our way to Leopold.

Outside Leopold, people were running helter skelter. There, I saw the bodies of two foreigners lying at the entrance. I couldn't believe my eyes—there was smoke everywhere and I could hear people wailing in pain. I had my gun handy, and stepped out of the back of the van. I'd put one foot on the ground when they opened the first round of fire, a bullet grazed my shoulder; a second bullet pierced my right palm—I fell to the ground. As I lay there, all I could hear was firing, screaming and then an eerie silence. Before any of us could even process what was happening—they'd disappeared in a cloud of smoke and were headed towards the Taj. As I was being driven to the hospital, I prayed hard. Not for myself, but for my city—I knew this was no ordinary attack.

VISHWAS NANGRE PATIL

9.45 P.M., TAJ My bodyguard Amit Khetle and I were on our way to Leopold when I got a second call from the DGP. He said there was firing and blasts happening at Taj; we rerouted to the hotel. Armed with one pistol each and no bullet proof vests—we entered Taj from the rear gate. There we met the Taj security chief Mr. Kudiyadi; the terrorists were mindlessly shooting, he led us to them. On the second floor, we saw three terrorists ten metres away from us. Fortunately, their backs were to us.

I saw an opportunity to kill them and took it—I fired three rounds. One of them was injured on the leg, but they sprayed AK-47 rounds on us—we took shelter behind a pillar. They disappeared.

We then scanned every floor until the 6th. We knocked on eight to ten rooms, but no one opened their doors. There was chaos in the air. Blood, bodies, the smell of gunpowder and intermittent firing—we had no idea where from. At that point we didn't know there were just four; nascent intel was that there could be upto 100 terrorists all over the city!

Until 11 p.m. it was a blind war; the Taj had gone into a deep silence. I thought they'd escaped, so we went to the main gate where four constables joined us. Just then, there were two blasts from inside—we went to the 6th floor. When we couldn't locate them, my batchmate Rajvardhan and I, who'd entered Taj by then, decided to go to the CCTV room.

On CCTV we saw three terrorists hitting five hostages and trying to get them down. I called the control room. CP Sir said, 'The naval commandos are coming in a few minutes; keep them pinned down.' On behalf of our team, I

said, 'We will not allow them to come down, even if we die.'

We began firing; they threw grenades and fired back—at 3 a.m. they set the dome on fire. The 6th floor was in flames. But we kept them occupied and 600 people were rescued from inside the Taj.

By then, they knew we were in the CCTV room. The electricity had gone and the room was filled with smoke. So we formed a chain and made our way out, but they saw us and sprayed us with bullets. Our team got split up. Amit was shot thrice; Rahul Shinde was martyred, Rajvardhan and I made it to Crystal Hall.

We had no cell phones, no walkies. We waited there until the NSG arrived after which we gave them the intel and they carried out their operation. Honestly, I was sure I wouldn't make it out alive. Even my family thought I was dead; they were preparing for my funeral—but I performed my duty and went home.

अरुण दा. जाधव
पो. ह. क्र. ८८/१५४२ मुंबई शहर

10.00 P.M., CAMA HOSPITAL That night, I called my mentor, Salaskar Saheb, and told him about the situation at CST. He called me to Colaba station. On my way, I picked up a sten gun. From there, as we were making our way to the control room, we got told that two terrorists had gone to Cama. We rerouted. At Cama I saw fifty cops—ATS team, crime branch police and Karkare Sir. Soon, Kamte Sir joined us. Just then, an officer drenched in blood staggered out of the back gate; he told us that two constables were dead and Mr. Sadanand Date was injured. Just as we helped him into a car, bullets poured down on us from above. At that point Kamte Sir picked up his AK-47 and fired. After that, Kamte Sir, Karkare Sir and Salaskar Saheb all sat in the Qualis; I sat at the very back. Along with two more operators and the driver, the seven of us set out. Just then, we got new information—in the Rang Bhavan gully two terrorists were spotted. Without informing the control room, we headed there. Salaskar Saheb dimmed the headlights, but the top light was on—Kasab and Ismail spotted us and hid in the bushes. As our car drove past slowly, they opened fire and threw a grenade.

Kamte Sir got shot in the head. Yogesh Patil fell on me; I shot three rounds and injured Kasab. They continued firing—three bullets hit me; my elbow was broken, my gun dropped to the floor. I was ready to die—I thought of my family, took God's name and waited for death, but my purpose hadn't been served yet.

11.50 P.M., METRO CINEMA They stopped firing and approached the car. Kasab threw Kamte Sir on the floor. He opened the back door and in a heavy northern accent said, 'Acha, jacket tha!' as he removed Karkare Sir's body from the car. When they reached Salaskar Saheb on the steering wheel, I thought he'd do something, but they threw his lifeless body on the floor. At that moment, the pain of the bullets was nothing—my mentor Salaskar Saheb was no more. Still, I was conscious and through the gap in the head rest, I could see them. Yogesh Patil was on me; he was still alive. But just then, his phone rang and on hearing that, Kasab randomly fired bullets towards the back seat. Again, I dodged death by a few millimeters.

As they drove past Metro Cinema and fired at the media and cops, the news spread that the terrorists were in a police vehicle. But at Vidhan Bhavan, the car broke down. So they got out of the car and stopped a Skoda—I saw them heading towards marine drive. That's when I called the control room and gave them all the information. After, a hoard of police officers found me in the Qualis—all their guns were pointed at me. I was in plain clothes—they could have shot me at any point. But luckily Mr. Parambir Singh's operator recognised me. I was hospitalised—for a whole day, my family had no idea where I was. I went into surgery, not knowing that in the days to come, I'd meet Ajmal Kasab once again.

12.20 A.M., CHOWPATTY News of the attacks were pouring in, when my senior inspector asked me to set up a nakabandi at Chowpatty. When I arrived there, Tukaram Omble and a few other officers were already present. We were sixteen men; two of us had pistols, the rest had lathis.

Around 12.20 a.m., we got the news that the two terrorists were making their way to Chowpatty in a Skoda. We decided to double barricade. At 12.30 a.m., a Skoda stopped fifty metres away from our nakabandi. We asked them to get out of the car with their hands up. They attempted to make a U-turn but their car rammed into the divider—they were now just two feet away from us. That's when Ismail fired two rounds. So, I fired three shots and another officer fired one. Ismail was gravely injured.

Kasab opened the left door—by then Omble Sir and his team had reached the car; they had lathis. Kasab lifted his gun—but Omble Sir caught the barrel of the rifle. Kasab fired—Omble Sir took seven bullets in his chest, but didn't let the rifle go. He fell to the floor with Kasab's AK-47 in hand. So I don't think I should speak about anything except Omble Sir and the debt that can never be repaid. I knew him for years—he trained junior constables. And on the day that mattered the most, he was fearless. With a lathi, he took on a terrorist with an AK-47; he gave up his life, but didn't let Kasab's gun go. That's the man he was—Tukaram Omble. Remember him today; remember him everyday.

OBEROI I was on my way home, when Mahale Saheb called me and asked me to rush to Colaba; he said it was a gang war. Within minutes, he called and said there's firing at CST and to rush there instead. Then another call for Oberoi. That's how it was that night. Finally, I was sent to GT Hospital to take the statements of those injured in the attack so we could gather intel.

But only dead bodies came in. First ten, then twenty, then thirty. And then I saw the sight that moved the ground beneath my feet—Salaskar Saheb's body was brought to the hospital. It was the worst night of my life. But we had one terrorist in our custody; there was no time to waste. We started collecting evidence. I remained on duty from 26 November to 5 December.

The conversations between the terrorists and their handlers shocked me. Fahadullah, the terrorist at Oberoi shot his hostages, whilst his handlers were on call. They kept repeating—'Save the last bullet for yourself; koi bhi halaat mein arrest nahi hona hain'. When I saw the CCTV footage, I teared up. A lady staff member at Oberoi with an injured hand ran into Tiffin to tell her guests to hide; a family with children hid under the table, but even they got shot. Later we found hundreds of bullet marks even on the floor. For ninety days, we worked non-stop on the charge sheet against Kasab. He was in my unit for forty-five days and every one of those forty-five days, he asked for just one thing—'Mujhe zeher dedo, mujhe goli maar do ... mein marna chahta hoon.

9.45 P.M., NARIMAN HOUSE I was outside Taj, when my informant called me and said, 'Saheb, Colaba pe blast hua hain.' I rushed to Nariman House. By the time I got there, one person was dead and the terrorists had thrown a grenade at the entrance of Nariman House. I contacted Maria Saheb and asked for manpower. The building lights had gone out and they were firing from the windows. So with my three men, I cleared the surrounding buildings.

Within fifteen minutes, 400 people were evacuated. My next agenda was to pin the terrorists down. By then, Maria Saheb had sent more men. We were eleven officers—we placed ourselves on different floors of the surrounding buildings and fired—we wanted them to know that the police had surrounded them. We then launched tear gas shells on them. By 5.30 a.m. more forces arrived—we had about 125 men. So we set up gonis through every road leading up to Nariman house to ensure there was no escape. They even tried coming down a couple of times, but we'd fire and they'd rush back up. As daylight approached, I wanted to storm the building. I called Maria Saheb to give me the go ahead, but by then we'd lost Salaskar Sir, Karkare Sir and Kamte Sir. He said, 'Bagwan I can't risk it, just hold; NSG will help you.' So we held our position for one and a half days until the NSG took possession on the 28th. And when I saw those bastards bodies after the NSG operation was complete, I felt anger. The way they'd kill their hostages was gruesome; what 'jannat' would take them? The deepest of hell is where they deserved to go.

PRESENT DAY A month after the attacks I appeared as the prime witness against Ajmal Kasab; it was on my statement, that he was hanged years later. Still, when I met him in jail, I couldn't control myself—I started beating him; at least ten cops had to pull me off him—I would have killed him with my bare hands. But God kept both of us alive so that I could testify against him and the roots of his terror were revealed to the world.

Looking back, years later I still remember every last detail. I've worn awards, the President has felicitated me and I'm back in service fighting crime, but I can't get over the loss of Salaskar Saheb—my mind goes back to how things could've been different; of how I could've saved him ... but I know that we were all soldiers that night and our first and only priority is the country.

So I'm on duty till today to continue to serve; my every breath is to ensure that the fifteen policemen, two NSG commandos and 149 civilians didn't lose their lives in vain.

MY MIND GOES BACK TO HOW THINGS COULD'VE BEEN DIFFERENT; OF HOW I COULD'VE SAVED HIM ...

I'VE BEEN A SECURITY GUARD at this girl's hostel for the last five years and I've lost count of the number of times boys have tried to sneak in through these gates! Every time. I catch them, they give me the stupidest excuses, like 'I forgot the way to my own hostel' or 'I was entering college from this gate'—there are no excuses I haven't heard before. But I take my job very seriously and till today, not a single boy has succeeded in sneaking in through these gates. Even when I'm having tea at the tea stall outside, I keep my eye on the gate and if I catch anyone trying to sneak in, just the terror of my loud whistle is enough to send them running! I know every single one of the 150 girls staying inside—they're all 'my girls' and as long as they're under my care, no boy is going to get entry—whether he's a boyfriend or some scoundrel.

SEEN IN
CHANDIGARH

IT WAS AFTER ONE CONVERSATION that we realized that being 'just friends' wouldn't work. On our first date, we went to CCD and sat there talking for three hours! After that, we texted all the time and met whenever we could—he was an aspiring cricketer and travelled a lot. Whenever he was in town, I would drop everything to meet him ... even if that meant studying less or ditching my friends. I had constant butterflies around him. He was my first relationship; my first love.

Somewhere at the back of my mind, I knew that being from different religions was an issue. But I was in love, so I let it be. We argued about normal 'couple' things, but looking back, I'm pretty sure I did most of the apologizing ... because I desperately wanted it to work.

Then the day came. I was dressed up for our college Traditional Day and was excited to meet him because I was looking good. But when I got to Candies, he told me we had to end it because of our religions and that his career came first. I sat there in silence. I remember feeling like my whole heart had been pulled out of my chest. I was so heartbroken that I didn't know how to function. I was so used to scheduling my life around him that I forgot how to 'be' without him. I cried whenever I thought of him, which was almost always. I isolated myself from my friends; I couldn't focus on my studies. I remember sitting at the table with my mom, when she asked me if I was fine because I was shivering. I broke down and told her everything—she just held me while I cried. Even my best friend would call me everyday. For the first few months, she travelled all the way to my house in Dadar to check-up on me. But, my turning point was when I failed one of the three papers I needed, in order to pass. I felt so stupid. How had I allowed a boy to determine not just my feelings, but my future? I needed to get my life on track and own who I was and what I wanted. One of the hardest things I did was delete him off all my social media profiles. I began focusing on studying, my relationship with my friends, and just the small things that made me happy.

BUT, MY TURNING POINT WAS WHEN I FAILED ONE OF THE THREE PAPERS I NEEDED IN ORDER TO PASS.

Finally, I cleared my exams and moved on. I understand why people say 'first love is the hardest'—but I don't regret it. I'm still a hopeless romantic, and believe that my soulmate is still out there. But I also know that loving someone wholeheartedly also means loving yourself first and that's what I'm trying to do right now ... to give myself the unconditional love that I've expected from others.

I WAS ON MY WAY to work from Mahim to Andheri when I got into Surender's cab. The entire ride, we made small talk about the weather, the traffic, and the city. I was eager to speak with him, because he wasn't from here and I wanted to know his story. He told me about his family in the village and how he was managing his income—keeping only a bit for himself and sending the rest back home.

By then, I'd reached my location and was rummaging through my bag; only to realise that I'd forgotten my wallet in my other bag. The bill was almost Rs 230, which is a big amount, even for me! I told him, 'Bhaiya, I've forgotten my wallet!' and started apologizing profusely. But the whole time, he was so cool about it! He just said, 'It's okay madam. We all make mistakes from time to time.' I was shocked—I expected him to be mad, instead, he was consoling me! He even told me, 'Madam, you're getting late for your meeting. It's alright—please go, and best of luck!' I took down his number and went for the meeting without paying. But all day, I couldn't stop thinking about his act of kindness.

Next morning, I called and asked him to meet me at the pick-up point. I paid him, adding a little extra to make up for the trouble he went through, but he didn't accept a single penny above 230! So instead I took him out for breakfast and we chatted about life as we sipped on some hot chai.

I haven't seen him after, but I always wish him well, because where he could have been angry and bitter, he chose to be kind and understanding. We're often so caught up with the big things, we forget about the little ones—the ones like these that make life beautiful. So go ahead—be that person today. Be kind; the reason someone smiles and thinks ... the world isn't so bad after all.

WHAT IS THE ONE THING
YOU LOVE THE MOST?
—FLOWERS!

I'VE RETIRED, BUT MY
HEART STILL DESIRES
TO DO SOME GOOD
FOR THE WORLD.

I'M SEVENTY-SEVEN YEARS OLD. I've never had any expectations that life was obligated to give me something in return. I simply followed the path laid out for me. I grew up in a family of five. We lived modestly. My father was working in a company and my mother was a housewife. I grew up watching them help people. They were always happy making others happy—always doing 'jalsa'—and this was something I wished to embody.

I was a good student in school. I got into my dream college too, but we didn't have enough money for the fee. So I changed my dream. I went to another college and started working to support my family. I was giving tuitions across the city—I'd cycle everywhere every day until late at night—proud because I was contributing!

Eventually, I got a job in a factory and had a stable income. But no matter what, I always saved up some money to give it to those in need. My family would complain at times that if I left with twenty rupees, I'd come back home with nothing because I was always compelled to give it away.

I still remember that once, I won a gold medal in a quiz when I was in school. It was my most prized possession, but during the period of the Indo-China war, I decided to sell it and use that money to give it to the defence fund. The army needed it more than I did.

In that moment, I was inspired by the people around me who were fighting for the wellbeing of others in an honest manner. Why only provide happiness to yourself when you can light up the life of more people?

So a few years ago, when my grocery store's helper came to me, telling me about how his son got into his dream school, but they didn't have the means to pay, he reminded me of myself. Everyone should have a chance to see their dream come true, no matter how small it is. I tried everything I could, spoke to everyone I knew, and got him a scholarship. He's just completing his graduation now. I'm so proud of him!

I've retired, but my heart still desires to do some good for the world, so I teach Vedic math, give books away for free, and still crowdfund for small local schools in villages. I don't do this for the shawls or the awards or the bouquets. I do it for the simple knowledge that someone else will relay the good further on and maybe ... just maybe, our country will be a better place. After all, 'you must be the change you wish to see in the world'.

THIS DIYA HAS REMAINED LIT FOR 600 YEARS NOW; three generations of my family have been taking care of it. This diya is a sign of prosperity. My husband would sit here and read the First Kalima. He devoted his life to this cause. We're Muslim, but people from all religions come here to pray.

My husband was really fit. He even used to work at the cotton mill in his younger days. But his legs gave up on him after a point. He was a blessed man though. Allah showed him mercy and gave him a great gift—he made him His messenger. Everyone would ask for his dua to make their wishes come true. And believe it or not, most of the time, they did!

But six years ago, he passed away. Now I sit here alone and do the things he used to do; it makes me happy. I feel closer to my husband, and like the flame, our love will never die out.

I USED TO LIVE IN A VILLAGE NEARBY—I lost both my parents at a young age. Life in India is tough for an orphan. You have no one to teach you how to earn, how to live, even how to survive. I would wander around aimlessly. As randomly as that, I came to this city in search of a job. A woman who sold flowers took me in, and taught me how to pick, tie and sell flowers. That was thirty-five years ago, and till date that's what I do.

I buy flowers from the market, tie and sell them at this exact spot without fail every day. Over the years, I've even made good friends here. They make sure I'm happy. Although sometimes they tease me because I'm dark, but I don't mind it much. As long as we're smiling and happy it's all okay sirji!

Reebok

MY PARENTS USED TO IRON clothes for a living and earned Rs 2,000 a month. We were three siblings and we struggled for basic amenities like electricity—we used to study under a street light.

Until class twelve, I studied rigorously. I got into one of the best universities and topped in the first year. I got a scholarship for the rest of the course. After, I was placed at my dream company and life changed for me and my family.

But fate had other plans.

On the night of my twenty-fifth birthday, I was travelling back home by train. I was standing by the door. That's when two men came and tried to steal my bag. One of them was holding me and one was pulling my bag. They then jumped off the moving train, taking me with them. They escaped but my left leg got stuck in the tracks. Four of the train's coaches ran over me and only then someone pulled the chain. I was taken to the hospital where the doctors had to amputate my leg. I was devastated.

For months, I was bedridden. But eventually, I got a prosthetic leg and walked a few steps for the first time.

I still had some lingering pain and when I visited the doctor, he told me that there were some staples still embedded in my leg that hadn't been properly removed. He said, 'You can walk. The staples won't harm you. But as it is, you can't run.'

I'M INDIA'S FIRST WOMAN BLADE RUNNER—I CAN'T EVEN EXPLAIN HOW IT FEELS!

That's when I realised that I'd never been privileged—I always had to work harder than others, so I had to do the same this time too. Hence I visited a rehab centre that trained para athletes—I didn't want to just walk through life, I wanted to run and prove everyone wrong.

I began training and pushed my limits. Soon, I was able to run! I even took part in a 21km marathon!

Now, I run marathons regularly and I'm India's first woman blade runner!

I know that there's not a lot of 'life' that is in our control. The next minute you live, can make or break your life. Your tomorrow could be the day that changes your life. But instead of taking those unexpected circumstances negatively, understand that it's nothing else but life giving you a chance to be a winner, all over again.

HIS FAVOURITE QUOTE WAS, 'DON'T WORRY, BE HAPPY!'—SO EVERY DAY, I WAKE UP WITH A SMILE AND TRY TO LIVE UP TO HIS MOTTO.

TRIGGER WARNING: SUICIDE I was ten when mom and dad told me and my sister, 'We're having financial issues.' I didn't understand what that meant, but I felt safe because we were together. Dad was a mathematician. He loved his work, and stayed up all night to get it done. I used to do all my homework with him.

He was an athlete and would run 5 km every Sunday! But over the next few months, dad got weaker and cried a lot. I'd smile and hug him, but after a few months, his condition worsened. Finally, he succumbed to depression and killed himself.

I clearly remember dad's side of the family telling everyone he died of a heart attack; only we knew the truth. Overnight, my entire life changed as we moved to Belgium—mom's home.

My aunt helped us find an apartment next to my grandparents and mom took up odd jobs to support us. It was difficult for her as she'd been out of the country for twenty-five years, but she always had a smile on her face and said, 'We'll figure it out'.

Every night my sister and I would fight to sleep next to mom, we were that shaken. But thankfully, we spoke openly about dad's death at home and mom even put me in therapy. For the longest time, I blamed myself; but therapy made me realise that dad's decision was his own and all I could do was accept it.

Still, there were days when I missed him terribly. Whenever I saw other kids complaining about their parents, I'd think, 'At least they have both their parents!' And whenever we had to fill forms, I'd usually turn in mine with just one signature, having to explain why dad was missing.

When I turned fifteen, I started working to become financially independent. I'd seen too much pain and trauma, caused by financial pressure. So, I'd be up by 7 a.m., go to school and study till 4 p.m., come back home and do homework, leave to babysit kids and finally reach home only at 10 p.m. On weekends, I worked till 1 a.m. as a waitress at a restaurant.

We were getting by fine, but I knew that further studies would be an issue. So alongside work, I studied round the clock and finally managed to get a 100 per cent scholarship! Mom was so proud!

I'm still studying and haven't figured out what I want to do. But I realised that while money is important, happiness is something that you can't put a price on.

So while I miss dad a lot, I know that he's in a better place now, free from all the pain. It took me ten long years, but I've finally made my peace with it. I remember, his favourite quote was, 'Don't worry, be happy!' So every day, I wake up with a smile and try to live up to his motto.

AS A CHILD, I USED TO GO to the Wular lake with Abbu; his job was to clean the lake. He'd tell me how important it is to keep the lake clean. Once, Abbu slipped from the boat and injured his leg When we took him to the doctor, we realised that Abbu had leg cancer and that the toxic lake water might have caused it. Within months, his cancer spread and he passed away.

Ammi wasn't well, so, at eight I dropped out of school and took Abbu's job. But I couldn't forget that the lake water was responsible for Abbu's death; I wanted to clean it. Everyday I'd collect 15kg of plastic, sell it and earn Rs 150 a day. Most of it, I'd give to Ammi and save the rest for my sister's school fees. I did this for seven years. Once, a kabadiwala told me, 'You've bought me 12,000 kg of plastic!' I was so happy, I wanted to do more.

So, I motivated other students to join me, in no time, we saw patches of clear water.

Word spread and in 2017, a documentary maker made a film on me! The Srinagar Municipal Corporation appointed me as the ambassador of cleanliness; even the PM praised me. Ever since, I've travelled around Kashmir telling people to respect our waters. It enrages me to see anyone throwing trash in the water; I give them a mouthful.

Over time, I saved up my salary and this year, I got my older sister married. Now, I want to buy a house for Ammi and send my younger sister to school. I want Abbu to be happy wherever he is. He was a good man and he died doing something we all should've been doing—keeping India clean.

NITIN AND I ARE COLLEGE SWEETHEARTS who entered the corporate world straight out of college and got married soon after. We often spoke about having a cozy house in the hills—we loved the outdoors. So whenever our 9-5 became 9-9, we'd get into the car and take off. We went where the road took us.

During one trip, we came across a hamlet on the bank of a river. The place was so raw—snow-capped mountains and a flowing river; I knew that this was the place we should call home; Nitin felt the same way. So, we evaluated our finances, took a loan, bought this piece of land and began building. I remember this one night, we were lying under the stars when Nitin painted a picture—swimming in our pool while sipping on fresh juices from our orchard. I held his hand and said, 'Some day.'

Coincidentally upon our return, we heard of a friend who'd died of a heart attack at forty-two! That was the last straw—we promised to move as soon as we could. We used up our savings and ensured that the kids' education didn't suffer. And after four years we finally relocated. This is our life now—we wake up early, drink spring water and have our meals by the river. I even find the time to paint. We wanted others to share our joy, so we started hosting guests from all over.

It's simple moments like these that I feel thankful for taking that detour. Because now, our 'some day' is 'today'. I've realised that it's futile to wait till you reach a certain age to do something, because not one person can ensure a 'tomorrow.' So what's the point of waiting or wasting even a minute?

I ONLY GOT TO KNOW MY HUSBAND after we were already married. After that, when we had kids, life became all about them and we forgot to treat each other as separate individuals. We planned our finances based on their needs, bought them new clothes even when ours were torn; even our meals were cooked based on their likes and dislikes. Still, we were happy.

When they grew up, I wanted them to leave the nest—didn't want to tie them down with the same responsibilities we had. So now, all of them are living their own lives. They have their families and jobs. They do visit us occasionally but now, it's finally just me and my husband living together. We've recently started to realize that both of us have changed over the years—we're almost completely different people! Suddenly it feels like we're newly weds discovering each other. We're finally getting the time to be 'alone', together.

I MAKE A ROUND TRIP TO AMRITSAR AND back every month; I'm on the road every day. It takes me ten days to go home each time, but I've been doing this for nineteen years. My wife and children are in Amritsar, I'm just coming from there but I already miss them. I was born and brought up there so I know everything there is to know about it, to know about home.

But, that's the transport business. You won't get a place to eat or rest and it leaves you with a deep longing for home. Ah, home! I wonder what chaos my kids are causing while I'm away. I can imagine my wife scolding them, saying, 'I'll tell papaji when he comes home'. But as soon as I walk in and they all come running to me, all's forgotten. Until it's time to leave again.

विजेता

MY TAYAJI STILL TELLS ME THAT when my brother first held me in his arms, 'He was on top of the world,' and no one had ever seen him that happy.

He had always wanted a younger sister and pampered me the most. He was my Tayaji's son, but we lived in the same house. He used to call me 'Silky' and never got bored of playing with me. Bhaiya was great at academics. Tayaji wanted him to become a doctor. But Bhaiya was sure—he wanted to join the Army and serve India, just like his father and grandfather. So, he cleared the UPSC entrance tests, started his military training, and in 1997, became a Lieutenant. I still remember watching him lead a parade—he was so happy to see me. He took me in his arms and introduced me to his friends—'She's my little sister who sends me postcards'. I used to scribble a few words on those postcards, and he cherished them. We had a large age gap and as a child, even though I couldn't express a lot, I loved him dearly. I would look forward to his letters and cry if he didn't come home for Rakhi.When the Kargil war broke out, he was posted in Gulmarg and led the Ghatak platoon. On 9 November 1999, the Pakistan Army launched an attack on his post. It was just three days before my birthday and I was eagerly waiting for his call. But instead, an Army officer called—Bhaiya was hit by a grenade and had suffered critical injuries. Tayaji burst into tears. The next day, we received confirmation that he had died fighting for the country.

I WOULD LOOK FORWARD TO HIS LETTERS AND CRY IF HE DIDN'T COME HOME FOR RAKHI.

His body was brought home on my birthday—a crowd had gathered outside our house. Even then, a distraught Tayaji said, 'My son kept fighting till his last breath, I'm so proud of him'.

Then, his belongings were returned to us—albums, uniform, his kada. The first photo in every album was mine. When he wasn't able to visit me, he'd ask for my photos and over the years, he preserved all of them. I stopped going to school for the next few months. It took me over a year to accept that I wouldn't see him again. My brother was just twenty-five and made an enormous sacrifice for his motherland, for all of us. He even won the Mahavir Chakra after, but no award can bring him back. After his death, our other brother left his corporate job to take Bhaiya's place and is serving as a Lieutenant Colonel in the Indian Army today. I speak to him two to three times a week. During the Jaisalmer sandstorm, when I couldn't reach him, I was terrified. When I finally spoke to him, I asked him to come home but he said he was fine and that duty comes first!

Every time I hear of a soldier sacrificing his life, my heart skips a beat. But as an army family, we already know how it is—for our jawans, India always comes first.

HONESTLY, WHEN ALL OF US nurses were called for service to the hospital to fight COVID-19, I was scared. I have two daughters and a husband at home, and I was concerned about their health. At that point, my 4th grader was naively just happy that her exams were cancelled, and my other daughter was paranoid that I'd catch the virus—she begged me to not report.

All I could do at that point was assure her that I'd be okay, because when duty calls, you show up—there's no plan B. So my husband took over the house and I left for work. Even getting to the hospital was a challenge, because travelling in a taxi was a huge risk. So my husband drove me, but that put him at risk. The other nurses and I decided to carpool, but soon we realised that it was best for us to just stay at the hospital. I still remember the first day—between admitting patients, allocating beds and calming down panicked patients ... it was like a war zone; we didn't even get a minute to rest. But the hardest thing we had to do was keep families apart. I was handling a couple from Pune who was begging me to leave to go home to their children—but I just couldn't let them leave. It was heart-breaking. I thought of my own children and how much I missed them. My daughters kept calling to make sure I had my mask on or was I eating, but even those calls lasted a few seconds.

There was so much to be done that we had to work extra shifts—we kept our morale high by sending each other motivational messages. One of the nurses left at 6 a.m. and returned at 9 a.m. because a new batch of travellers had arrived—she worked until midnight again that night. But all of this is worth it when we see the look of relief on our patient's faces when they test negative.

Just last week this group of travellers literally thanked us with folded hands for taking care of them. In these situations, I always just say that it's our first and only duty to serve. These are trying times, but we will get through them together. Believe only credible sources for information, take our instructions seriously and please stay at home.

Help us by not getting out unless it's for essentials or if there's an emergency. And once this is all over, we will all celebrate. You celebrate with your friends and family and we nurses will celebrate with ours—we can do it together, by just being at home.

"AND ONCE THIS IS ALL OVER, WE WILL ALL CELEBRATE. WE CAN DO IT TOGETHER, BY JUST BEING HOME ALONE.

I'VE LIVED A VERY DIFFICULT LIFE. I ran away from home when I was seven, because I didn't want to be a burden on my poor father. I fell off from a running train and lost my leg. When the doctors asked me about my parents, I lied and said I was an orphan—that became my new reality. I was sent to an orphanage, but the situation was so dire, that I ran away again, this time to beg on the streets.

As luck would have it, I got caught by the cops for begging, and was sent to juvenile jail. There, I met a boy who would sing beautiful qawwalis. I was so fascinated by his songs that I immersed myself into learning Urdu and Hindi.

When I got out, I made my songs my livelihood. I would pen down shayaris in every free minute. But the growing hustle and bustle of the city made it impossible for me to continue. I had to resort to begging again. Then one day, the Gods smiled at me. They sent me an angel in the form of a girl—this girl who saw an old beggar, but thought he was worth talking to. She was distributing sweets for her grandfather's barsi, but she ended up talking to me for an hour and reading all my poetry. She visited me frequently after and then managed to take me to the Spoken Word fest where I performed for the first time for twenty-two minutes! They were the best twenty-two minutes of my life. She then took me to more events where I performed my Shayari, and much to this old man's delight, people loved it!

Not only did she introduce my words to the world, but she also raised enough money to help me to set up a book stall. I no longer have to beg and it's all because she cared enough and because Allah wanted to prove to me that angels exist—especially in the darkest of times.

**I GAVE MY HINDI EXAM TODAY
AND TOMORROW IS MATHS.
—OH! HOW WAS IT?
I DON'T KNOW. MAIN BHOOL GAYA!
—AISE KAISE?
I WAS WRITING AND THEN I FELL ASLEEP!
WHEN I WOKE UP,
TEACHER TOOK MY PAPER AWAY!**

ITANAGAR

I'VE BEEN A GARBAGE COLLECTOR since I was ten years old. Every day I separate the wet and dry waste and then discard it accordingly. My earning depends on whatever I've collected during the day. I don't get a fixed salary so there's no question of getting a pension—I can't even think of quitting. I work seven days a week, 365 days a year. Even during festivals when everyone is dressed up and celebrating, I'm still sitting in garbage. I know someone has to do this work and I don't mind being that someone. I'm used to it after all these years.

The only thing I'm asking in return is a bit of acknowledgment—when you throw something on the street, remember that it doesn't just disappear; there's a person at the end of the chain who is taking care of your trash. I've gotten hurt by broken glass and even bloodied my hands from menstrual pads. I'm not complaining, I'm just asking you to think of me before you litter the next time.

THE TOILS OF TIME

EVER SINCE I WAS BORN, my favorite place in all of Hassan Abad, Kashmir, was Ammi's lap. There, I felt the safest. Twenty-five years later, lying on the cold, hard floor of Tihar Jail, I'd crave nothing more than to feel her arms around me.

My happiest memories go back to my childhood. We were four brothers and four sisters. I was the third child, but the most pampered! Every time I did well in school, Ammi made my favorite paneer sabzi! Abu was my idol. He worked at his government job during the day, and spent his evenings at our carpet shop. Seeing him work tirelessly, taught me ambition. After school, I'd run to our shop and learn the ropes. I still remember the thrill of my first sale; I clutched on to those Rs 48 all day! When I grew older, I took out a loan to source material. I'd wake up at 6 a.m. everyday, and sell carpets at the market. By sixteen, I was financially independent; Abu was proud—he helped me start my shop. I even fell in love with a girl I wanted to marry. But suddenly after I turned eighteen, Kashmir was no longer the Jannat I knew; it became a battleground.

Military vans roamed the streets, the sound of gunshots would startle us at odd hours and we'd receive news of Kashmiris being killed daily. We were scared to leave our homes. Hundreds were extorted for 'chanda.' Still, we kept working. But one day, on our way to the shop, Abu and I were stopped by a military van; six men with guns interrogated and threatened us to stay home.

The violence increased; curfews were imposed. Of the forty-eight classmates I had in school, thirty had been killed. With no savings or income, Abu warned me and my brothers, 'If you want to live ... leave Kashmir.' Overnight, my brothers and I said goodbye to the only home we'd known; we had to earn for the family. Ammi was howling; she refused to let go of my arm, but I promised her that I'd be back soon. We caught a bus and hoped to make it to Delhi alive. We made it and got a small room, but even before we settled down, police officers busted down our door to interrogate us. They didn't have a warrant, but we were Kashmiri, and that was enough for them to be suspicious. They incessantly asked; 'Why are you here?' 'What are your connections?' We had only one answer; we are simple men, trying to make a living. Eventually they left, but we were on their radar.

For the next one and a half years, the police tracked our every move. Every other day, they'd bust into our room asking why we were late to come home on a particular day, or where we'd gone another day. If we ever had a visitor, the

FOR THE NEXT FIFTEEN YEARS WE WERE SPIED UPON, THE POLICE TRACKED OUR EVERY MOVE

police were alerted and sent to interrogate them. Our landlords felt harassed and forced us to move out. We were thrown out like that often because wherever we went, the police followed. It was hard to work with them breathing down our necks, so when I heard of the booming carpet business in Nepal, my ears perked up. I talked to shopkeepers and saved up enough to move with one of my brothers. On the way, we stopped in Kashmir and again, I promised Ammi that I'd be back soon. In Kathmandu, we weren't Muslims or Kashmiris, we were just human. Our business was picking up; I thought the worst was behind us. Until one day, when we were talking about my marriage plans with my beloved, we heard a knock on the door.

TRIGGER WARNING I opened the door to see police officers from Delhi and Nepal. Before I could utter a word, they barged in and put us in handcuffs. We begged them to stop, but they pointed their guns at us—we sat in their van and did as we were told. At the Nepal Police headquarters, I saw about 400 panicked faces; they'd rounded up all the Kashmiris in Nepal. No one knew what was going on. The police confiscated our belongings and questioned us—I was terrified. They showed me pictures of different men; one man looked familiar; 'That's Javed bhai from the carpet business in Kashmir!' I said, not knowing I'd just spelled my doom. I was thrown into a van with two others, while my brother was detained in Nepal. Next to me was a fifteen year old boy named Naza; he banged at the windows out of fear, but they slapped him so hard, we all kept quiet. A day later, we were in a special cell in Delhi where they held terrorists. They constantly asked me, 'Who was responsible for the Lajpat Nagar blasts?' I didn't even know that such a terrible thing had occurred, but they thought I was involved because the man who I'd identified was the suspected mastermind behind the blasts—I was accused of being his ally.

For the next fourteen days they mercilessly tortured us—they electrocuted me till I vomited, beat us with Lathis till we bled, and pulled apart my legs in opposite directions till I screamed. I couldn't even walk; I had to crawl to the bathroom. I grew so afraid that when they asked us to sign a blank paper, I did it blindly. They told me that I'd be able to go home soon. But the next day, we were produced in court and upon their order, thrown into Tihar Jail—my family had no idea where I was. Then, when an older Kashmiri inmate heard my story, he said, 'Beta, tujhe buri tarah se phasaaya gaya hai.' I wouldn't wish life in Cell No. 3 of Tihar Jail on my worst enemy. Locked up in a 10x10 foot dark cell, I was made to sleep on the hard cement floor; inches away from the latrine. My skin crawled at the stench as rats picked at my shit. We were treated like animals—at 6 a.m., we were woken up with a loud bang and given watery dal and roti twice a day. We were only allowed to leave our cell for thirty minutes; those moments were my solace. I grew close to Lateef and Naza, the two other suspects—we kept each other going.

I cried everyday thinking about my family—I wasn't allowed to call them. We weren't given bail or even a lawyer in the early days—I didn't know that was my right.

Every fourteen days, we'd be taken to court and I'd think, 'This time they'll set me free'. But then I found out that the blank paper I'd signed was turned into a charge sheet of false confessions. I'd been framed as a terrorist responsible for the Lajpat Nagar bomb blast.

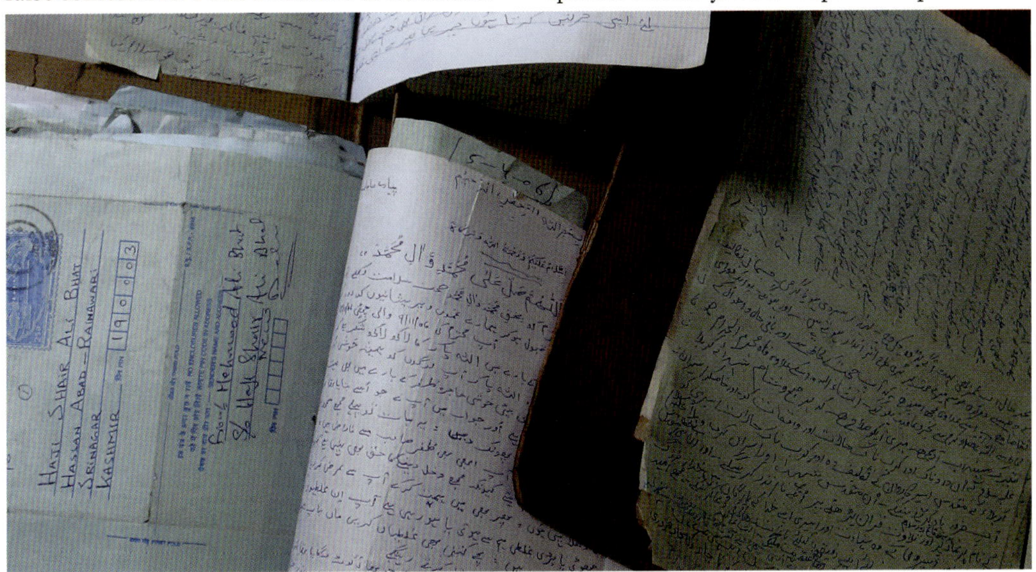

Then our names were dragged into the Samleti blasts in Rajasthan, and we were moved to Jaipur Jail. For nine months, we weren't let out of our cell or even allowed to shower.

When we were moved back to Tihar Jail, an officer let it slip that we'd be there till they found the real criminals; we were scapegoats.

Thankfully, my family finally got word and Abu rushed to Delhi. Once, I was leaving court, when I looked up and saw him crying profusely. He asked, 'Did you do it?' I cried and swore that I didn't—he believed me. After that, I wrote to them—they were my only reason to live.

My family did everything they could to pay for a lawyer; Ammi and Abu spun yarn and my younger brother gave up his studies to earn. When Ammi heard that I didn't have soap, she sent me Rs 600 and said, 'This is my blood, sweat and tears—spend it carefully.' I didn't spend a Rupee.

After four years in jail, a letter titled 'Emergency' arrived. When I read it, I fell to the ground—Ammi had died. My beloved wrote that it was from the heartbreak of losing me; she called out my name on her deathbed. She was just fifty-five and I didn't get to see her one last time; she couldn't afford to visit me in jail. I wept till I ran out of tears. A part of me died with her, and with the losses that were to come, my heart felt like a graveyard. Fourteen years passed; I began to feel like I'd been born in jail. And that I'd die there. I'd been sentenced to death in Delhi's trial court. And four years later, I got life imprisonment in Rajasthan's trial court; for crimes I didn't commit. That's when advocate Kamini Ji came into our lives. She'd heard about us in the news, and told us, 'I know you're innocent. I'll fight for you.'

All the while, I struggled to hold onto memories from before. My days melted into years, but even as my hair turned from black to grey to white—time stood still.

Letters from my family were my only piece of home. I'd read about Eid, sisters getting married and having children. I found out that the girl I loved since I was sixteen, had been married off to another man.

My brothers visited me once a year; we'd talk to each other through the netted jaali for thirty minutes.

Meanwhile, the trial in the High Court moved at snail's pace; I was convinced I'd only go home for my burial.

Inside jail, the attendants were monsters. They'd find any excuse to thrash me every other day. Once, they filled my chai with salt, and when I refused to drink it, I was beaten. They would hide letters from my family. Other inmates made us massage their feet and threw rocks at us. I kept quiet—those who spoke up got beaten so badly that they had to be hospitalised.

Then in 2011, the Delhi high court acquitted us, but we were moved to Jaipur—our second trial was yet to begin.

In 2015, I lost Abu too; I was orphaned in jail. But even in the worst of times, there's hope. At the time we had no idea what was going on with the case. We stopped going to court; either the bench of judges had changed, or they'd drown us in dates. We'd accepted our fate, but almost as suddenly as we'd been arrested in 1996, our case took a sharp turn.

In 2019, Kamini ji faced a new bench of judges. I don't know what had been missing in the last twenty-three years, but this bench was

convinced of our innocence within two days! We got to know the night before, when the warden told us, 'You're being released tomorrow'. I didn't believe them.

But when the release order arrived—Lateef, Naza and I cried and hugged each other. twenty-three years later, we were finally free.

At 5 p.m. on 23 July 2019, we stepped out of Jaipur jail. I looked up to the sky as I took my first breath as a free man. My brother hugged me; I broke down in his arms. But when you've been a prisoner for so long, freedom can be hard to accept. On our way to the airport, I kept checking if we were being followed.

When we landed in Kashmir, one hundred and fifty people gathered to see me. But the first thing I did was rush to my parents. I threw myself at their graves and screamed, 'Mein wapas aa gaya!' I kissed the mud and hugged their grave thinking that if I tried hard enough, they'd hug me back.

I cried inconsolably—they died with their last wish unfulfilled of seeing me free.

Everything felt strange. I couldn't recognize anyone except my siblings. For a few weeks, we all lived in one home and I rested my head in my sister's lap only to miss my Ammi more. They introduced me to my nieces and nephews and everything I'd missed.

But it was hard. I couldn't sleep on a bed because I was used to the jail floor. I'd have nightmares of being back in that cell and wake up drenched in sweat.

It's been nine months, but when I look in the mirror, I see a stranger. I'm a forty-nine year old man—the past twenty-three years stole my youth, my parents and the life that could have been. I came out of jail with no apology or compensation.

All those years, I wasn't living; I was existing. But I don't want to waste a second of my freedom anymore; I'm on borrowed time. I want to work. I want to marry someone I love, raise a family, and find that young man within me, who was once full of dreams. I want to say I'm alive ... and mean it.

HAVING SPENT TWENTY-THREE YEARS IN PRISON, I wanted to find that young man within me, who was once full of dreams. When my sister said, 'You need a companion,' I froze—the last time I'd felt love was thirty-three years ago. I didn't know if I'd be able to love again. Moreover, why would anyone want to be with a forty-nine-year-old man like me? As expected, three women rejected me. Then came Fatima Ji's rishta. I can never forget the day I met her—she was dressed plainly and didn't talk much. I asked her, 'Fatima Ji, apne itne saade kapde kyun pehne hai?' Her reply stole my heart, 'I don't want you to be deceived by outward appearances,' she said. We spoke for four hours—I told her about my life in Cell No. 3. She told me about her failed marriage—she'd left her husband because they were demanding dowry. Through our past suffering, we connected. I told her, 'I might not be a charming prince, but I promise I'll do everything to keep you happy.' She replied, 'Aadhi roti khayenge toh bhi mehnat ki khayenge; saath me khayange.' Our wedding date was fixed—I wanted to spend time with Fatima Ji. So, I got permission from her Abbu and took her out—we'd stroll around Dal lake and eat ice cream. Ek din maine chupke se bol diya, 'I love you Fatima Ji'; she went red! We had a small wedding soon after; I call her Fatima Ji in public, but when we're alone, I call her Jaan and she blushes! Faatima Ji has brought so much happiness into my life; it feels like a dream. Three weeks of marital bliss and I'm already starting to forget the pain of twenty-three years. It's true what they say, 'Love heals you.'

I OPENED THIS SHOP FIVE YEARS BACK ALONG with my husband and two sons. We are originally from a small village in Karnataka, but there was no scope or job opportunity to earn even a third of what we earn right now. So we decided to uproot ourselves and move to this new city.

We used to be farmers back home; the scanty rains left us with no choice but to sell everything off and leave to fend for ourselves. To add to this, my elder son died last year due to jaundice and I have to take care of his wife and two kids as well. My younger son helps me at the shop too, so we are trying to support each other in every way we can.

All I wish is for my grandchildren to study well and be educated, and accomplished in life; to not have to work like us. I want them to achieve a lot more than I can even dream of.

"WE USED TO BE FARMERS BACK HOME, BUT THE SCANTY RAINS LEFT US WITH NO CHOICE BUT TO SELL EVERYTHING OFF.

I WAS JUST OUT OF COLLEGE and excited to work, when my health went for a toss. Suddenly I began throwing up and fell so sick that I couldn't even get out of bed. The doctor said I had a tumor around my ovaries and they might have to be removed. She asked me, 'Do you want kids?' So Renvin my boyfriend goes like, 'What will I do with the kids if she's not well? Keep them in the cupboard?'

I knew it was his lame attempt to make me laugh, but it worked. And right before the surgery, he asked me to flash my biggest smile. The surgery went well and I was looking forward to going back to normal life, when I got the biggest blow—I had cancer. I broke down. At twenty-one, you don't expect to hear that—ever. Renvin was abroad for work and kept shuttling a lot. So when I called to tell him, he just said, 'Rach. Who's the winner?' And like a little kid I told him, 'I am!' And I felt better again.

My chemo began shortly after—it hurt like hell. My sessions were five days straight and the dosage was high. Every part of my body hurt, I couldn't eat much and was in bed all day. The effects started right after the first session. One morning, I was combing my hair and an entire lock fell into my hand. I was scared seeing that much hair! So I asked my salon aunty to come home and chop it all off. Oddly enough, after she did, I felt so strong; I felt like I could do anything! That evening, when Renvin came home and saw me, he just said, 'I'll be back with groceries.' Instead, he returned with a shaved head and said, 'I'm with you every step of the way!'; I was so touched, I hugged him and cried. Over time, I started recovering—on days when I didn't have chemo, I was doing an online MBA or chilling with my friends. The environment was so positive that if there was ever a low moment, someone was right there to pick me up. Even when I had to undergo blood transfusion, I wasn't as scared because everyone just kept me going. Five months later, the doctors declared I was cancer-free! When I told Renvin, he celebrated with his colleagues at work and shouted, 'Who's the winner Rach?' And I happily said, 'I am!' Few months in, I still wasn't allowed to go out much. But when Bryan Adams came for his concert tour, Renvin took me with every precaution. When my favorite song came on, he got down on one knee and asked, 'Will you marry me?' My answer was a resounding, 'YES!' I don't even have the words to tell you how I felt. I remember, my heart was beating so fast, but there was no uncertainty—I always knew he's the one for me, for better or for bald!

I ALWAYS KNEW HE'S THE ONE FOR ME, FOR BETTER OR FOR BALD!

SURF TOUR 68
NEW SHAPES
REVEALED

> WE COME FROM DIFFERENT WORLDS BUT A GIRL FROM THE UK HAS FOUND HER SOLACE IN AN AUTO DRIVER FROM UP—NO MATTER HOW MUCH PEOPLE JUDGE US, THIS IS A PRETTY GREAT FRIENDSHIP.

I MOVED TO MUMBAI FROM THE UK a few months back for a fellowship. When I was coming back home after my first day at work, every auto driver rejected me. It was frustrating but then Aajam came, and finally agreed to take me home. Throughout the journey I initiated conversations about his life and livelihood, and I found him really interesting. I didn't see any reason not to start a conversation!

By the end of that ride, I asked him to be my regular auto driver. We exchanged phone numbers and I asked him to meet me at the same time and location every day.

For some reason, I felt really comfortable around him. So, within a few days, I started opening up to him. I discussed my life with him—I just got really good vibes from him. But somehow, he never said anything. He thought it was odd to get 'comfortable' with passengers.

But still, he started looking out for me. I remember I had to attend a friend's party one night—and he agreed to come and drop me to the location safely. I asked him to go back home, but he insisted that I wouldn't get a ride back and actually waited for three hours to take me back home! I think that was the start of our friendship.

All of my friends and family know him as one of my closest friends in Mumbai because I meet him every single day, and talk to him about everything. When I tell people about him—they warn me not to trust an 'auto driver'. But honestly, no one knows Aajam the way I do.

I've also forgotten my phone a few times and when he returns it to me, he scolds me like an elder brother to take care of my belongings. He's also helping me with my Hindi and I'm teaching him English ... I've even promised to take him to London with me one day! Now, we're going to open a bank account for him so that he can get his finances in order.

We come from different worlds but a girl from the UK has found her solace in an auto driver from UP—no matter how much people judge us, this is a pretty great friendship. And I can't wait to send you guys our selfie from London!

WHAT'S THE BEST PART OF YOUR DAY?
—MY AFTERNOON NAP!
WHAT'S THE WORST PART OF YOUR DAY?
—WAKING UP FROM MY AFTERNOON NAP!

I WORK AS A SECURITY GUARD at a college nearby—I check every student's ID card before they enter. Not many people appreciate and respect what we do, but I do get some students who go out of their way to be kind! Some students have gifted me money on my birthday so I can go out and eat to celebrate, while others give me gifts on random days. This one time, a girl came up to me and touched my feet because it was her birthday—it made me so happy! I don't know if any of the students who see my face will ever remember me. But there are a few special ones whom I will never forget—because even though they didn't need to, they still brought a smile to my face.

MY FATHER'S FROM TAMIL NADU and my mother's from Burma. When I was young, we got onto the last boat that was leaving for Chennai and crossed over. Ever since, we've been making a livelihood here; it was my father's idea to sell Burmese food in Chennai and eventually I took over. Today, after almost fifty years, we're still the only people making burmese cuisine in North Madras. Chennaites travel kilometers to come here and eat our food, especially the noodles! They also click photos like you—to put on that 'graam'!

CAN WE TAKE YOUR PHOTOGRAPH?

—QUICKLY QUICKLY, BEFORE ANYBODY SEES ME! WE'RE NOT ALLOWED TO GET PHOTOS CLICKED HERE. BUT I LOOK NICE TODAY, SO I'LL ALLOW YOU!

IT HURT ME TO KNOW THAT I'D JUST PUSHED HIM OUT OF MY LIFE, WHEN I WAS SO MADLY IN LOVE WITH HIM.

WE MET FOR THE FIRST TIME through a common friend at a party. I was already in a long-distance relationship, but when our eyes met, we knew that there was something there. We met a few more times, and my friend told me that he'd started to like me, but I was already dating. He's a Bohri Muslim and I'm a Hindu, so I also knew that it wouldn't work. My parents live in Oman, and one day I was really bothered about issues at home, and issues with my then boyfriend. I needed someone to talk to; without a second's thought, I called him home. He came over, and just listened to everything I had to say. That night, something changed. I was much more attached to him than I realised. We spent a year and a half after that, still as friends. At the time, my relationship with my then boyfriend was becoming very toxic for me. So, when I couldn't take it anymore—I broke up.

That's when Hakim and I became closer. We'd meet each other every single day of the week, and still didn't get bored. I knew I was holding back, but I was falling in love. He felt like a breath of fresh air, and he added that extra sunshine to my life.

But I knew that because of our religions, it wouldn't work. So, before I got too attached, I decided to cut all ties. I met him one last time, and said that I wouldn't be in touch anymore.

But after I came home—I fell horribly sick, I couldn't sleep and it hurt me to know that I'd just pushed him out of my life, even when I was so madly in love with him. The next morning I told him that I regretted my decision, and that I wanted to spend my forever with him. He felt the same way. And that's when our love story started. It's been over a year since we've been together. His parents accepted us with open arms, and while it took some time, when my parents saw just how happy, secure and loved he makes me feel, they agreed too.

Being with him makes me feel like the luckiest girl in the world. I realised that true love finds you in the most unexpected places, makes you go through hurdles that you never think you'll overcome, but it saves you when you need it the most, and shows you just show beautiful the world can be on the other side.

ON MARCH 20TH, I got a call from my team saying that I had to pilot a rescue flight to get 263 Indians trapped in Rome back to Delhi. I had five seconds to give my answer, and all I could think about was my five-year-old son and eighteen-month-old daughter. But the thought of those 263 Indians desperately waiting to go back home to their families made me agree. I left the next day, kissing my kids goodbye. When my crew and I boarded the flight, there were no passengers; just eight hours of silence. But after the passengers in Rome boarded the flight, the vibe instantly changed; it felt like the pandemic never existed. After landing, the passengers cheered for us. A passenger even said, 'I never thought a flight home would mean so much'.

After what felt like a rescue mission, I headed home. But when my son ran to hug me as I entered, I had to tell him, 'Mumma can't hug you'. When my baby girl saw me, she waddled her way to me—but my husband had to take her away. She screamed and cried—it broke my heart. I had to isolate for fourteen days; in those fourteen days, my daughter would try sneaking into my room. It became a game, where I'd run and she'd try to catch me. It was the best way to explain the situation to my baby. But after isolating, when I finally got to hold my kids, I felt what those passengers must have felt—an ache to be close to your loved ones. And if it means that we can bring families together, I'm ready to pilot as many flights as it takes to bring my fellow Indians home.

ABHYUDAY AND I HAVE ALWAYS known each other. He's even in a few of my kindergarten birthday pictures! Years later, we bumped into each other at a concert.

I ended up at his place for a house party after, and the first thing I said to him was, 'Can I wear your slippers?' To top it off, I left the party without thanking him. I did leave the slippers behind though—a twisted Cinderella moment! A few days later, Abhyuday pinged me on Instagram and we met up for dinner. We started spending more time together; everything just naturally fell into place. I think it was sometime in January, that Abhyuday decided to talk to my parents; he didn't want to pop the question without informing them. He concocted this elaborate scheme and told me that we were doing a staycation at a hotel. But when we got there, he said that an uncle of his had come to meet us. So there I was, dressing up for an uncle I had never even heard of. But when I reached the deck, every single one of our friends were there; all of that was a blur. I could only see Abhyuday in front of me, and nothing else. He went down on his knees and asked me to marry him—I screamed, 'YES!' Knowingly, unknowingly, we knew each other through so many phases of our lives. The Universe was showing me signs all along, and thank God I noticed them—sooner rather than later!

WHEN I WAS IN THE 9TH STANDARD, I started an NGO called 'Denied', to help those who are denied their rights, like sex workers. Since then, I've always wanted to do more in whichever way I can, so when I moved to Bombay for college, the first thing I did was to look for an NGO to work with. When I joined one, I didn't like the way they spoke to children, so I decided to explore slums myself. I live in Santacruz and visited a slum right by my house—I was shocked to see that kids who were going to school still couldn't read or write. I decided to begin there—I began going to the slum every day and working with the kids. Every day they would ask me, 'Didi story sunaoge na?' and I would concoct stories on the spot—it was so worth it when I saw their bright, smiling faces! I began adding morals to these stories and noticed that slowly, they picked up on what I was trying to teach them! I even began taking them to my house for a change of scene. I still remember this one time, they broke a flower pot at home by mistake. As I began cleaning the mess, they handed me a paper that read, 'Sorry Didi'. I forgot all about the flower pot because my kids had perfectly spelled everything on that paper! I spent every single day with them—either learning or just being with them while they played.

NO DEED IS TOO SMALL, NO KINDNESS IS EVER TOO LESS.

I remember how, this one time I had taken them to the beach and was just lying down, enjoying the sunset when Laxmi, one of my students, came and sat next to me. When I asked her why she wasn't playing, she said, 'I can't leave you alone—you aren't playing with us!' They became my family, but a while ago their slum was demolished. I remember being present at their meetings, trying to help them negotiate things when one of the resident's there said, 'No outsiders should be allowed', obviously referring to me. But that's when Ganesh Bhau, the leader of the slum, said, 'She's family, she stays'. I had tears in my eyes. I wish I could have done more to help them.

Now my kids are dispersed all over the city, but I still try to meet as many as I can through the week. I know there's still lots more to be done. I set out with the intention that even if one child benefits, I would have made the world a better place—and that's all we need to remember. No deed is too small, no kindness is ever too little.

MY HUSBAND IS THE MOST EXTROVERTED PERSON YOU'LL MEET, while I'm the opposite. Every day after work, he forces me to chat with him. The only time we probably even fight is when I talk less and he gets annoyed that I don't have anything to share with him. One of these days, I'm going to figure out how to be as chatty as him all the time! But the only time that happens is when my favorite actors' movie releases, which he hates; we're opposites in that too! But I think our differences are what keeps the relationship alive. We argue, we fight, but then we apologize and make up. The making up is the best!

WHAT'S THE BEST PART OF YOUR JOB? Even without snooping, I can always tell that it's a love letter. They nervously snatch the letters from me before their parents can get their hands on it! Like many other kids, I grew up watching human beings oh so eager for the postman. On many occasions and other days, the postman would bring life changing news. And then, we grew up and everything around us changed. Letters are merely bills and other documents now. Technology has taken over and so people are not curious anymore I guess. But yeah, I am finally a postman now. Nervous woman waiting for letters from their loved ones and making sure they do not get busted at home and many such events, it happens all the time! A postman is truly the closest to so many families, strangely enough, we might just know it all, even without peeping into your letters. After all, we carry them to you!

MAA GREW UP IN A CONSERVATIVE FAMILY and was married off at the age of eighteen. Since then, her life has revolved around us. Papa would be away for work, so Maa would play both roles despite her blood pressure issues. She would cook , drop us to school, take my brother for cricket training, drop me off for dance class ... all while managing the household and finances. She did it all with a perpetual smile on her face. I'd never see her rest. She's always multitasking, almost like she has ten hands like Maa Durga.

Even during Durga Puja, she'd wake up at 4 a.m., partake in a three-hour long ceremony, prepare meals for everyone whilst keeping a nine day fast. But now that we've grown up, we help her with daily chores. So, with some more free time, Maa decided to realise her dream of becoming a designer; a dream she sacrificed twenty-two years ago for our family. It was time for a role reversal. We'd stay up late to help her with her designs—she started with traditional suits and sarees. And when she made her first sale, we surprised her with her favourite food and set up karaoke. We sang Lata Di's songs all night. Eventually, we helped her tie up with ecommerce websites.

She's starting over at the age of forty—but if there is someone who can do it, it's Maa. Often, we overlook the role of our homemakers—it isn't 'just cooking' or 'just picking and dropping the kids'—it's their whole life ... and my Maa is no different. Whenever life demanded, she gracefully essayed the role of each of Maa Durga's nine avatars; but I know today that she's first and foremost the 9th Goddess—Goddess Siddhidatri, the giver ... and I'll never take that for granted.

WE MET AT A MUTUAL FRIEND'S wedding and danced together the whole night! The next day, I woke up to a message from him, saying, 'Are you okay?' and in my head, I was like, 'What happened to me?'. He'll deny it but it was his way of starting a conversation! We started hanging out and he grew to become my best friend. I remember, I was studying in London when he asked me, 'What do you feel like doing for your birthday?' I said, 'I just feel like being by the ocean'—the next morning he sent me tickets to Mykonos and said ... 'Let's go?'

We've always been this way—and while most of the world saw that there was more than friendship—it took us a while. I mean we've dated other people, stopped talking and then became friends again, until I stopped talking to him for three weeks because I told him that he couldn't take me for granted. He called me after those three weeks, and said, 'Out of the 100 things I want to do in life, I can imagine doing 99 of them ... only with you.' After that he did whatever it took, but what melted my heart the most was seeing how he got over his lifelong phobia of dogs ... to take care of mine. I'm Muslim and he's Hindu so it took us some time to convince our parents, but through it all he made one thing clear—we would get through it together. In a time when religion still plays a major role when it comes to choosing life partners, Aman chose me. And, I fell in love with someone who does not make me feel like I'm hard to love! The past six years have been madness, but when the time was right I finally understood why I had to wait so long, and why he's been worth that wait.

I WAS ASKED IF I CAME FROM A CIRCUS WHEN I WAS SIX. I dreaded every new batch of kids that joined school; it meant they hadn't seen me before and I'd have to bear their reaction. I'd cry to my teachers and parents; my parents are dwarfs too. They'd cry with me because they felt like it was their fault. Over time, the comments became, 'Tujhe kaun milega?' I liked my best friend but when I told him, he said, 'My parents will never accept you.' My own friends would say, 'You should settle for anyone.' The real trauma began when my dad started looking for grooms for me. I met around thirty-two men, out of which twenty-five said no, and the ones who said 'yes' said I'd have to make a lot of compromises because of the way I looked.

I REFUSED TO SEE MYSELF AS DISABLED FROM THAT DAY.

One family came home and told me that if they had money, they'd never marry their son to someone like me. This other family entered our home, looked at us, and just burst out laughing. After several failed meetings, I gave up. I'd fight with my dad—I'd tell him we were enough for each other and we didn't need a groom. I wanted to distract myself, so I worked hard at my job and began attending charity events for the disabled. There, I met this man who was partially blind. He asked me what disability I had. When I told him I have small limbs, he said, 'But you have limbs, right?' He couldn't believe that I thought I was disabled. Talking to him changed my perspective.

Soon after, I met Mark, who was also a dwarf. We got to talking and he invited me to play badminton with him. We'd play regularly and then more people with dwarfism started joining us. We started writing to brands about hosting marathons and brands agreed to sponsor us! I wanted the world to know about us, so I wrote to TEDx. They were equally excited and that's how I gave my first TED talk! There, directors of a TV game show found me and told me that they wanted me to come on their show! It was after the show that people started recognising me. From the 'small girl', I became 'that girl from the game show'; that was a big deal for me—I felt human! I felt more confident about myself and wanted to give love a shot again after my dad died last year. But this time around I knew I wasn't going to settle—I wanted a kind, educated man. And in a few months, I found someone! When we spoke, he told me he thought I was too good for him because of how much I'd achieved. We met and connected. We're engaged now and getting married soon! Never let anyone tell you that you need to settle. Don't settle.

I WAS FIVE AND BADAMI JI WAS THREE when we got married in Azamgarh, UP. The only memory I have of the ceremony is of her hair being tied in a braid; she looked like a doll. We thought we were attending a party—we got to wear new clothes and eat ladoos. We had no idea we had been married off. So, when we did meet, we'd reunite like old friends. As we grew older, the responsibilities of being 'pati' and 'patni' became clearer; Badami Ji came to live with me at the age of twenty-one. Our friendship slipped into love before we knew it—we'd grown up together and known each other our whole life. We knew from the start that we didn't want our children to have the same fate as us. So when I held our daughter for the first time, I decided to leave UP. We packed our bags and moved to Delhi in 1961. Here, I became a fruit seller. I would leave early in the morning to get fruits from the mandi and Badami Ji would set up the stall. In the afternoons, Badami Ji would take over; she was a better saleswoman than me! Eventually, as our family grew to five, we began selling vegetables—we had our fair share of good and bad days. But we'd keep going for the times when we could afford chai and biscuit from the nearby tapri. My favourite day is Friday though ... because on Fridays, Badami Ji makes aloo baingan!

As our kids grew older, we opened a chai stall. Initially, it took a toll on us financially, but Badami Ji had faith in me and my cooking. I remember asking her,

THERE IS NO 'AADMI KA KAAM' OR 'AURAT KA KAAM' IN OUR HOUSE; 50-50 PARTNERS HAIN HUM!

'Nahi chala toh?' She smiled and said, 'Koi baat nahi, kuch aur karengey!' I wouldn't have had the courage to do anything without her. She may look small, but she has a strong willpower! So, in 1990, after hitting a half-century, we started Baba Ka Dhaba! Badami Ji does the chopping, while I prepare the dishes. There is no 'aadmi ka kaam' or 'aurat ka kaam' in our house; 50-50 partners hain hum! But after lockdown, our business suffered. We were barely scraping by—the food we cooked was going to waste and we had run out of money to buy vegetables. Lekin waqt hain, badalta rehta hain—out of nowhere, a stranger came to our Dhaba, took our video ... and the next day, we woke up to a line outside! Since then, all news people, company walas and customers have been coming and going. But when you were talking to Badami Ji just now, I overheard her saying, 'Dekho iss umar mein bhi kitni mehnat karte hain!' Yeh toh best compliment hua na, madamji?

I'VE BEEN A HOUSEWIFE ALL MY LIFE. But I've always wanted to do more. I love driving anything and everything—from two-wheelers to cars to lorries. But that's about it. Nothing came out of it until recently, when an opportunity knocked on my door that matched my passion to a profession. The job was for a Swiggy delivery executive—I took it up without even thinking twice. I deliver food to every doorstep. It makes me feel so empowered to be financially independent. I'm one of the few women delivery executives in Chennai, and I'm proud to admit that I haven't let anyone use my gender as a way of stopping me. Plus, I get lots of compliments on how I look riding my scooty—so that's another bonus!

I'M WELL INTO MY SEVENTIES, but I still work as a rickshaw driver. Over the years, I've witnessed the world transforming—everything around me is constantly changing. But I'm a man of routine. Every day, I take a break for an hour and sit under a leafy tree with my newspaper. I make sure to read it from start to finish—it's my tradition. As the chaos of the world continues, this is my piece of sanity.

LADY JUSTICE

I WAS BORN IN A VILLAGE CALLED UGGARPUR in Uttar Pradesh. Until recently, even if you googled it, it wouldn't show up—that's how remote the place is. When my mother found out she was pregnant, she wanted to abort me because they already had three daughters and three sons, but we couldn't afford it. When she delivered me, a girl—everyone was unhappy, except my father and bua. The elders and my mother even contemplated killing me. 'What will we do with one more girl?' they asked. Thankfully, bua and papa intervened and I got a shot at life.

While growing up, my brothers treated me like an unwanted child. Things got better eventually, but I always felt that us girls weren't treated equally within the family.

But, my father gave me the space to grow independently—that's why even though I was just five, I fought to go to school which was one km away from my village. We had to make our way through a jungle patch to even get there, but somehow the seven of us—all girls—managed together until the 8th grade.

After that, all the girls from my class dropped out—the senior school was three km away, and no one from our village wanted to send their girls so far. 'For what?', they asked. 'She'll get married soon anyway—no point spending money and sending her so far.' But I was stubborn. By then my father had become the village Pradhan and I would see city people and MLAs visit him with their educated children. 'Why not me?' I asked. I'd also read books on Indira Gandhi and Rani of Jhansi and wanted to become like them. I asked my father that if my brother's studies weren't being stopped, then why mine?

Finally, my teacher, Mr Jagdish Tripathi met papa and convinced him to let me study further and that's how I became the first girl from my village to study beyond the 8th standard. But my father was worried about my security, because it took me nearly three hours each way. He realised a little late that he had nothing to worry about, because when this one boy tried to pass cheap comments and get closer, I beat him black and blue. A crowd gathered and that guy started apologising, but I said, 'Mein chodungi nahi tujhe!' Word spread. These boys would say, 'Bahut dangerous ladki hain, usse panga mat lena, who seedhe maarne lagti hain'. My intolerance towards inequality and patriarchy started since then, but maybe it was just in my destiny to go through all of this, so that one day I could fight the most important case of my life to get justice for Jyoti Singh Pandey ... Nirbhaya.'

I was so excited to study further that I didn't care about much else—I put on my worn-out slippers, carried my jhola, took my brother's cycle and went to class. I took part in everything—I gave speeches, and even got chosen to captain my NCC team in Lucknow—again everyone in my village opposed this. 'She'll go to the city and ruin our name', they said, but my father supported me. I took money from my brother and without telling anyone, left for Lucknow. There, we won the competition and my name came in the paper—a small article about a village girl leading her team to victory. After that, for some time, I was left alone.

But after 10th class, my family insisted on my marriage. I was so scared of my studies being stopped that I went on a hunger strike for three days! The ladke wale heard about this, got scared of this 'pagal, ziddi ladki' and didn't even show up to see me!

I was desperate to study. To pay for my college fees, I sold my paayal and earrings and started teaching at a school. Throughout all this, I just refused to give up. Even in 2002, when my father passed away and my eldest brother said, 'Now no one will pamper you, you have to get married', my friend Rinky helped me get the LLB form and books. Finally, I left home.

This has been my life—taking up jobs, sometimes walking to get to class, sacrificing food and sleep—just so that I could become a lawyer.

But let me tell you, the status of women lawyers in Bombay or Delhi is different from that in smaller cities. In Kanpur, we were given no respect in courts—it was common for a woman lawyer to not get dates just because of her gender.

So eventually, I moved to Delhi, where I began preparing for my UPSC exams.

I was staying in a PG when it happened. 16 December 2012, the day they gang raped her in a way no one could fathom. When we woke up to the news; there was fear and anger. twelve girls from my PG immediately left Delhi because their parents were terrified. I was gutted. I cried uncontrollably as I thought about her; about what she went through. When more details started pouring in, something in me moved. I wiped my tears. All my life, I'd fought for myself, but this wasn't the time to sit at home and cry—it was the time to get out there and fight back.

The whole country became aggressive. She went through torture that we can't even imagine—we all felt the pain. At that point, had any of us seen the accused, we would have shred them to pieces—such was our frame of mind. Where we were housed, there were around 50,000 young people in and around the area—we decided to protest.

On 22 December, I was at the forefront of the protest at India Gate. I'd climbed a pole to tell the crowd that we needed to fight to get her treated out of the country. They sprayed water cannons on us, lathi charged us, but we didn't stop. I attended every protest from beginning to end. I can't explain how I felt when we got the news that she had succumbed and lost her life. I felt so deeply connected to her that I organised a meet in her memory and invited her parents. After that, there's rarely been a day that I haven't spoken to aunty. I also followed the case like a hawk and attended every hearing, even though I wasn't Jyoti's counsel.

I made sure I was present on 7th of January, when they filed the charge sheet in Saket court. There were a few lawyers there who wanted to take the case of the accused—I appealed to them on moral grounds to not take it. I knew it was illogical; the accused had to go through due process—but I was just so angry.

That's when AP Singh jumped in and took the case of the accused, while the state provided a lawyer to defend Jyoti. Over the next year, the convicts were sentenced to death in the District Court. Still, there was no execution. Months went by and aunty grew sadder with each passing day. To add to everything, when a journalist had questioned AP Singh on whether he would have taken the case, had Jyoti been his daughter, he said, 'If she was my daughter, I would have poured petrol on her and let her burn'.

My blood was boiling. Finally, in May 2014, when I spoke to aunty, she said to me, 'I don't think my daughter will get justice'. That's when I promised her, 'I'll fight for Jyoti; I'll take the case—hum chodenge nahi unhe.'

TRIGGER WARNING I still remember the way I felt when I saw the convicts in the High Court. I was gut-wrenched—images of their brutality and crimes haunted my mind. But they behaved as if nothing had happened; they joked with each other and even dared to smile at aunty—they just didn't care. I was filled with a rage like never before. As a woman, I wanted to beat them and make them pay with my own hands for what they did. But as a lawyer, I had to put a stone on my heart and keep calm. Through a flurry of cross-examinations, witness statements and DNA testing, I saw all four of them lie through their

teeth. Vinay and Pawan said they were at a party that night; Akshay claimed he was out of town, and Mukesh said he was just driving the bus and didn't rape her.

The bite marks on Jyoti's body matched Akshay's teeth. The skin in her nails was theirs and samples of their sperm were found in her private area. I can't put into words what I felt when they produced that rod in court. I felt like I would faint, even imagining the pain that it would have caused her. Still, they lied and said they hadn't seen the rod before. Their fingerprints were all over it.

Even after the High Court passed the death sentence, AP Singh amped up his aggression to save the convicts. He verbally attacked judges in court, delayed the appeals to stop the case from moving forward and even took to insulting Jyoti's character. I was shocked. I saw my opponent for what he was—a prejudiced man who would stop at nothing. As much as his words triggered me, I knew I couldn't flinch. I needed to understand his mind-set to defeat him. So, I kept my composure no matter how much he tried to rile me up and fought with dignity.

Still, justice was nowhere in sight and the matter wasn't moving forward. As much as I tried to comfort uncle and aunty, they had lost hope. But I swore to them that as long as a death penalty was in the letter of the law, justice would be served. My fight wasn't just for Jyoti anymore, it was for every girl in India. I was ready for anything that came my way. Even if that meant fighting my first ever case in the highest court of India—the Supreme court.'

It was tough for me to even get a date in the Supreme Court—I desperately tried to get our matter heard, but in vain. The courts had a backlog of pending cases and I was even told that our case wouldn't be heard before 2021. But how could this case be ignored? I made calls to advocates, aggressively pushed the registrar's office, and finally got a hearing after one entire year. Two years and eleven months after that, in 2017, the Supreme Court gave the same verdict—the convicts deserved to die.

But AP Singh tried everything to delay the final execution. He drowned me in countless petitions. Every time I won a round, there were ten others that hadn't even begun. He had found his loophole—the convicts were to be hung together or not at all. So, even though he could have filed petitions for all four of them together, he chose to file each one after the previous one had been dismissed, prolonging the trial and our agony. It was a vicious cycle that led nowhere.

Every day they lived was another day of justice denied. It had been six years at that point. Why were the courts being so lenient? Had they not seen the rod that still gives me nightmares? Hadn't they heard the nation's outrage? Or had we just normalised rape, no matter how brutal?

Justice felt distant, but I found the strength to push harder, every time I went to Jyoti's room and saw a photo of her smiling. You know, after everything the only thing she told aunty in the hospital was that she wanted to live? That she wanted to see her torturers hang and become a doctor to help others?

I kept looking at her photo and promised her that I would make sure they hang—to prove that she did nothing wrong that night. That her being out at 8 p.m. with her male friend didn't give those men a right to rape her and take her life.

I became relentless. I wrote letters to the President and Prime Minister, I questioned the delay aggressively in the media and fought in court like my life depended on it. It didn't matter that it was my first case—for every ounce of experience that AP Singh had, I made up for it by just not giving up.

Finally, seven years, three death warrants and countless delays later, our efforts paid off. Justice for Jyoti would be delivered on 20 March 2020—the four of them were finally going to hang. But AP Singh hadn't given up yet—he had another trick up his sleeve.'

The night before the hanging, while India slept, I was in court. After trying his luck in the lower courts, AP Singh woke up the Supreme Court at 12.00 a.m. in a last-ditch attempt to save the convicts. An emergency session had been called.

I watched as he scrambled in front of the judges. He tried using old arguments, made baseless accusations and even tried to use COVID-19 as an excuse to delay the execution. At that point, I didn't even need to fight back; the court was tired of his antics and saw through them. Finally, at three in the morning, the judge said, 'It's time for your clients to meet with God and you need to accept that, AP Singh!'

But he still couldn't accept it. Outside the courtroom, he abused Jyoti in front of the media and blamed her for the suffering of the convict's family. He asked, 'Pawan's mother is handicapped, Vinay has a young son—who will look after them?' When a journalist asked him, 'What about Jyoti's mother?', he said, 'What about her? She didn't even know where her own daughter was that night!' We didn't even bother responding—he had lost the war.

At 5.30 a.m. that same morning, as aunty, uncle and I watched the news of the hanging at Tihar jail, we hugged each other and cried. We had finally won—Jyoti's soul could rest in peace.

It's strange ... I'd never even met Jyoti, but I felt attached to her as if she was my little sister. She could have grown up to do such amazing things for the world, had she survived.

We fought for over seven years, but we still have a long way to go, because the mentality is still the same. After they were hung, I began receiving threats on my social media handles. They abused me and said things like, 'We'll rape you worse than Jyoti'. I don't care about those comments, but what pains me is that ever since, I've received over 500 messages from women—some send me pictures of the FIRs they've filed to no avail and others tell me about how they've been raped, harassed or violated without any justice. I'm going to reach out to all of them to say, 'Hum chodenge nahi unhe'. The fight has just begun.

HAVE YOU DONE A READING FOR YOURSELF?

NO, NO. JUST LIKE A DOCTOR DOESN'T PERFORM SURGERY on himself, or a barber doesn't cut his own hair, I only read for customers. In fact, my son is studying to be an engineer; I don't encourage him to take up astrology either. It won't earn him enough. With every passing day, people's belief in this is decreasing. I don't blame or judge them for it. I have total belief in my work and I do it with dedication. I can't make others believe if they don't want to. You see, faith is something that has to come from within. It loses its whole purpose if it's forced. So, I press on with my own faith, that all those who truly need me, will be brought my way; I don't need to do anything to make that happen.

I WAS BORN IN A SMALL TOWN, and had nine siblings. So growing up, we had limited means. I had never travelled, or even taken time off. Things changed when I got married. My husband and I only met on the day of our marriage. And one of the first things he asked me was if I had travelled. I told him that I didn't even have a passport, but he said, 'We've got to make you one, because together, we're going to travel the world.'

Both of us had very hectic jobs—but we decided to travel at least twice a year. Our first trip was to Darjeeling, where we went for our honeymoon. I remember we were on the bus, when it started raining very heavily. The window was open so the water kept coming in. He saw that and tried to shut the window—but ended up breaking it in the process. The entire bus was full, so we had to sit for twelve hours with the rain water spilling onto us! By the time we reached, we were totally drenched, but we just laughed it off!

We've been to places like Kathmandu, Shimla, Delhi. We've had to sleep on our suitcases because we've missed trains and we've had to spend hours stranded in the middle of nowhere because our buses have broken down. But it's all been worth it! This one time we were on our way to Badrinath, but midway we realised that the path ahead was blocked. It was late evening and there was no way we could drive back. So our tour guide arranged our stay at a local's house.

The area around was so eerie, I was really scared, and the whole night we could hear a weird sound—it was like somebody was outside. But in the morning we realised that it was just the sound of water hitting the rocks! When we grew older, we dreamed of travelling to Europe and even started saving up for it. We'd use every free minute to read books and research Euroepean cities! But suddenly I was diagnosed with breast cancer—the doctors were hopeful and so, I started my chemotherapy. But he was really scared of losing me. For the five years of my treatment, we left everything and went to Europe—for us, it was now or never. We travelled to London, Netherlands, Belgium, Austria, Germany, Switzerland, France, and even Italy! Once I was completely cured of cancer, we decided to use our savings and go to every country we've dreamt of going to like Australia and Russia. We plan to visit at least one country every year. On the day we first met, he was a complete stranger, but now he's the man of my dreams. Life with him has just been amazing. I never thought we'd fall in love, and when we did I never thought that our love would take us around the world. He never fails to surprise me and I couldn't have asked for anything more than a lifetime of new experiences with him.

ON THE DAY WE FIRST MET, HE WAS A COMPLETE STRANGER, BUT NOW HE'S THE MAN OF MY DREAMS.

I SAW HER FOR THE FIRST TIME before Dussehra—we were neighbours. But because I was away at boarding school, we never met. In 1976, when I came back to Raipur, I remember her vividly. She was wearing red—we were both flying kites on our terraces. That first glance was the beginning of everything; for the next two years, we'd keep trying to catch a glimpse of each other. But back then, even that felt like a crime, because she's Muslim and I'm Hindu.

Finally, she wrote me a letter where she called me by my pet name 'Chunnu' and told me she liked me. For three years, we wrote hundreds of letters to each other. I couldn't live without her—whenever she was out of town, I'd sit in one place for hours and wait for her to come back.

Times were different back then, even when we went for a movie, we took our friends along. Once when we spotted a neighbour, we left midway! We kept meeting with friends after that. But once her brother saw us ... and everything changed. She got a big firing at home.

So I went to talk to her parents, but they politely asked me to leave. I told my parents as well—their reaction wasn't good. By then, I'd set up my business and was renting two flats for work. I was a planner, and had some money saved up.

I told her I wanted to marry her. She was scared, but we were so much in love that it was beyond our control. We spoke to our parents but even though they'd known each other for years, our religion came in the way. Our fathers met once and decided—'Dono ko samjha lenge'. We had no choice but to elope.

SHE WROTE ME A LETTER WHERE SHE CALLED ME BY MY PET NAME 'CHUNNU' AND TOLD ME SHE LIKED ME.

On our wedding day, she left for college normally. From there, we went to Arya Samaj, got married and immediately left for Nagpur. We'd written letters to our parents and asked our friends to give it to them only after we reached Nagpur. When we returned to Raipur, we moved into one of the flats I'd rented for work. Her father came to meet me—he said only one thing, 'Take care of her.' My parents came once too. Still, relatives taunted us—my uncle even said he'd get me married again. Even when we found out she was pregnant two months later, the rumors continued—people said that we got married because she was already pregnant.

We ignored everything, but when our daughter was born, we left Raipur. We wanted to live a peaceful life. We moved from city to city after, and finally settled in Goa—by then, we were a family of four! Through our forty-four years together, religion has never ever come up—we celebrate all festivals at home; puja and namaz alike. I'm a pure vegetarian but everyone else eats meat. We respect each other's faith and beliefs. That's why we decided to name our home 'हम'—H for Hindu and M for Muslim. Because there's no space for religion in 'हम'—there's just love ... there's just us.

हम

ALWAYS REMEMBER, 'CHALTE CHALTE HI MARNA HAI!'

I'M GOING TO TURN 100 IN THREE MONTHS and my daughter is going to make kheer for me on my birthday! It's not easy to be a person who has lived for so long ... I've seen a lot. I've had to live through the death of my sons, one who was an alcoholic and the other who had a heart attack.

But still, life moves on. So, all one can really do is keep moving to keep up. Always remember, 'chalte chalte hi marna hai!'

THAT'S THE POWER OF THIS GODDESS— YOU CAN SEE HER THROUGH MY SMILE.

MY ENTIRE FAMILY HAS DEDICATED their lives to God. My mother, my brother and I, carry around Mahalaxmi. This is our purpose—we are the messengers. I know not everyone believes or even listens to what I have to say, but I manage to get many donations because of my smile. That's the power of this goddess—you can see her through my smile.

IN 2015, MY WIFE AND I WERE SAVING up to go on a peaceful and 'just us' holiday to Australia ... little did we know that our fund was going to soon be eaten, and I mean literally eaten by our unexpected arrivals! We were in the 3rd month of our pregnancy when we realized my wife was pregnant. The surprises didn't stop there—our first sonography showed that we were expecting twins—you can only imagine the sheer terrifying excitement! I planned on staying at home while my wife went back to work, it was an obvious decision—she earned more and we now had an army to feed. When I first told my dad about my decision of staying at home, he only asked me once if I was sure—when I said yes, he never asked me again. It was harder for others to understand—questions like 'Lahar, are you going to be comfortable asking your wife for money?' or 'Are you really going to be at home while your wife is at work?' or 'Are you really going to do housework?' were thrown my way. I was always good at responding to these questions with the obvious truth. Thing is, my wife carried them for nine months, she has this unique bond with them that no one in the world will ever have. So it's only fair that I bond with them too! But kids keep you always moving on your feet, and with two of them, I was running ... Eat, poop, sleep became our mantra! Like most kids, mine slept for about eighteen hours at various intervals, but I had two who were never in sync—so I was at a new level of sleep deprivation. My sense of depth was completely out of whack—I cannot tell you the number of times I have walked into something that was right in front of me! I remember our feeding schedule—post-its stuck on the wall after either of us fed a kid, just so we could keep track. Obviously, there have been multiple times where one of us has fed one kid, forgotten to update our post-it wall, and the same kid has been fed again ... It's a running joke between us that we don't remember the months of March and April 2016 ...

I PLANNED ON STAYING AT HOME WHILE MY WIFE WENT BACK TO WORK, IT WAS AN OBVIOUS DECISION FOR US.

Our memories of those two months are all just a blur with these two rascals. But nothing will be more special than that time I had with them—the diaper changes, the all-nighters, the crying fests. Surprisingly, when one year down the line, I decided to go back to work, the transition was smooth. My wife and I both work now, and raise our kids together. It's always family first for us—how does it matter who's the one providing and who's staying at home? My wife is happy, I'm happy and the rascals are most definitely happy ... I don't think anything else should matter!

... BECAUSE THE CLOSET IS MEANT FOR CLOTHES, NOT FOR YOU AND I.

I DIDN'T HAVE A HAPPY CHILDHOOD. My mom killed herself when I was in the 3rd grade and after she passed, dad would drink every night and abuse us. At school, I was a fat kid with no friends. Studies didn't interest me, but I was creative.

So I got into arts college and things changed—I lost weight and made a lot of friends. I even had my first relationship! One day, my boyfriend made a move on me, but I felt so weird, I ran away. Soon after I took up a photography course—that's where I met her. She was so affectionate, she made me feel all fuzzy—I was crushing on her! I never told her, but came out to a cousin, who asked, 'Are you sure about this?' When I said yes, she hugged me and said, 'If you need anything, I'm with you.'

After the course, I got a job as a photographer and soon, I came to be known as 'The Funky Girl'. And as work took off, I earned enough to move out. At work, I was open about being gay, so when a journalist asked for an interview, I agreed. The day the article came out, dad was really mad and we didn't speak for days. But there was a silver lining—a few weeks later, a girl texted me saying she was a huge fan.

We started chatting, which turned into phone calls and one night, she asked me out. I immediately said yes. I was falling for her too! We were together for six years and were really happy. But her parents didn't know about her and she'd refuse to even hold my hand. It broke my heart, but I ended it.

I felt it was time to tell my story and so I created a photo series on the closeted life of a lesbian couple. It went viral and got featured in US and Mexico! And last year, I did another photo series on struggles faced by transgenders. When Vice picked it up, I was so happy I couldn't stop crying! People have even told me that the series helped them come out to their parents. Over the past few years, I've patched things up with dad too. Although he won't say it, I know he's proud of me—for doing this all by myself.

My life's been pretty much about giving others a platform to be themselves. Because the closet is meant for clothes, not for you and I. Because all of us, no matter what our gender, skin color or sexual orientation, we're human. Because at the end of the day, all we need is a little love.

YOU CAN FIND HAPPINESS EVERYWHERE ONLY IF YOU REMEMBER TO MAKE THE LITTLE THINGS COUNT.

IN EVERY SITUATION, I TRY TO ENJOY MYSELF AND KEEP SMILING. I'm a tour car-driver— driving from one place to another can be tiring, but still, there are so many happy moments to look forward to. Once, I was taking a car full of tourists from Bombay to Goa! As we were driving, they played some English song—even though I didn't understand much, they made me sing along and join the fun. Eleven hours seemed like eleven minutes. I laughed so much during that entire trip, as if I'd known them for years. So I guess you can find happiness everywhere only if you remember to make the little things count.

I WAS TEN, WHEN ONE DAY I WOKE up to see a bunch of my hair on my pillow. Then, when I combed my hair, more fell off. Days passed and I started observing bald patches on my head, often. My parents and I consulted several physicians but none of them were able to diagnose my condition. Finally, we found a doctor who could tell us what was wrong—I had Alopecia. But we had no idea what the cure was. Every passing day I saw my hair fall off, along with the confidence I had, my parents supported me but it was hard for me to accept reality.

Things got worse when my vacation ended and I had to go back to school. Students started bullying me—even teachers would give me weird stares. There were days when I'd lock myself up in the bathroom and cry. I remember this one time, I was invited to a friend's birthday party and wanted to wear this really pretty dress. But I was so scared of going, I thought people would judge me. I didn't want to be made fun of. But that's when my mom told me that, 'It doesn't matter what people think of you , they'll ridicule you anyway—so do what makes you truly happy!' It was a simple sentence, but so empowering.

With hesitance, but a little hope—I wore that dress and decided to go to the party. That's when I realised that it didn't matter what people thought of me—the fact that I had accepted myself, made life better. A few years later, when I was in college, I found a doctor in Kolkata who promised to treat my condition. It actually made a difference. I slowly started getting my hair back. But I was living in Bangalore at that time, so each time, I had to travel all the way to Kolkata. That was taking all the energy out of me. I realised that I was putting so much pressure to be a certain way, when I was actually at peace with exactly how I looked. That's when I threw my medications into the trash and shaved my head. I'm thirty now, and even today people ask me if I have 'cancer' or if I've shaved off my hair because of a 'religious belief'. I still stand out amongst the crowd but it just doesn't bother me anymore. I'm living life the way I want to. When I look in the mirror, I don't see any flaws, I wear a pair of earrings to match my confidence. Because for me, life isn't about the things that I don't have, or things that I may lack—it's about owning my beauty, irrespective of whether it matches anybody else's standard, or not.

I TRULY ACCEPTED AND EMBRACED MY IDENTITY. I'M LIVING LIFE THE WAY I WANT TO.

WHEN MY COLLEAGUE DIDN'T TURN UP FOR A MEETING, I called to check on her. 'I'm sick, I had to go back home', she said. When I probed further she said, 'I got my period and didn't have a pad.' So I got to thinking—thousands of women are probably kept out of work, school, sports because of this 'issue'. Why aren't pads available in public toilets? So the next day, I bought twenty packets of sanitary pads. After taking permission from local authorities, I went to a public toilet and kept pads there. When I told Maa, she said, 'I'm so proud of you; take money from Papa also.' Over time, I started charging Rs 2 for each pad. Seeing me outside a women's toilet, men would yell, 'Are you gay?' I ignored them. After a few months, I started conducting menstrual education campaigns in villages. Often, I'd be the only man amongst hundreds of women; girls would hesitate to talk to me. But eventually, they got comfortable and shared their problems. I then made a documentary on menstrual hygiene. While conducting interviews in a village, when I asked , 'Who'd go to the doctor for a vaginal infection?', a young girl said, 'We don't have lady doctors here.' That hit me hard. So I set up medical camps for women. Within one year, I built dispensers across fifty public toilets in Kolkata. This year, I developed an app where you can track the nearest washroom with a pad dispenser. There's still miles to go and the biggest hurdle is changing the mindset. A woman's period isn't a hush-hush matter ... She bleeds five days a month, every month. The least we can do is talk about it.

WHEN I WAS YOUNGER I had many dreams for myself. But I had to drop out of school and fend for my family. I'm twenty-one, and every day I ferry passengers who are close to my age. I see them all dressed up—going to college or work. I see them living their best life. Meanwhile I'm struggling daily, just to put food on the table. And the people on the road, and my passengers, don't make it any easier. This one time, I was riding my auto when a lady overtook me. Her car got slightly scratched and she got so angry. In the middle of the road she started arguing and calling me all sorts of names. She even threatened to take me to the police station for no fault of mine. I couldn't help but wonder whether she would've spoken to me like that if I was a well-educated man and not just a rickshaw driver. But this is my life now and I've made peace with it—not all of us can get what we want. Some of us just have to sit back and watch, while others chase their dreams. But I still hold on to the hope that maybe, one day, somehow, it'll be my time to shine.

I WAS TWENTY-ONE WHEN I GOT MARRIED; I was fresh out of college and was a child of a single mother who had been raised by her grandparents. My marriage was into an extremely rich family, and I was coming from a completely different background altogether—of meagre financial stability and a complete lack of anything to do with fashion. My husband was the quintessential Punjabi man who wanted a trophy wife. I would always be made to feel small, not good enough. He'd have a problem with the way I dressed, he'd always compare me with other women who were taller and prettier and he'd constantly tell me how I was not beautiful. I ended up feeling miserable and tried tremendously to save my marriage from falling apart. Within months of my wedding, I conceived. But it only went from bad to worse. Because of this, I started to get suicidal thoughts—within eight months I knew I could not take this anymore and that I had to get out of that prison because I did not want my baby to grow up in that atmosphere. I still remember, I got out of that house with only a bag and some Rs 28 in my pocket, never to return again. Arjun was born four days later. I still remember, when he cried for the first time, I asked the nurses why they were making him cry. That is what I wanted for him—to never cry, to always be happy. Little did I know about how I was going to make that possible. I had no financial aid from my family and I had to make ends meet as well as provide for my son. I took up odd jobs like being an assistant in a company because I had no qualifications except my bachelors. That

I'D GROWN UP WITH MY GRANDFATHER ALWAYS TELLING ME HOW WE MUST NEVER LEAVE OUR SPIRITS.

is where I met Piyush—we'd often cross each other but would never really talk. I was fighting my own battles and not looking at anything else. But, a few months later, Piyush and I met again through a mutual friend and that is when we sort of understood that we liked each other. He slowly and gradually became my support system. I was still lost in life and did not know what to do. But he slowly started telling me how I was capable of so much—he pushed me to study fashion because I was always drawn towards my aunt who was a fashion designer. I'd grown up with my grandfather always telling me how we must never leave our spirits. He had prepared me well before all of this happened to me and I was glad that I was ready. So, amidst all this struggle I knew I was the tigress who had her cub and hence, everything was going to be good in the jungle. There would be days when I'd go to the court and my ex-husband would threaten me. I would feel utterly helpless but I never let any of that get to my spirit.

The case started in 2009 and ended in 2016—7 years I struggled to get my baby with me and I won the battle of good versus evil.

I'M A CELEBRITY HAIRSTYLIST NOW. A LONG WAY FROM A KID WORKING IN TATA. I'VE EMBRACED THE PART OF ME WHO LOVES ART AND CULTURE AND I'M EVEN A NUDE MODEL NOW.

THE WOMEN IN MY LIFE HELPED ME become the best version of myself. Everyone around me noticed that I was a little different. So, my family and I were asked 'Why is he like this?' a lot. How could I tell them? When even I didn't know? Growing up, I had no idea who I was.

I thought my attraction towards men was a phase and I always thought that I would go back to being 'normal'. In college, I was made the cultural head of my fest. During that, I found my best friend. She was the co-head. We spoke about her body image issues and I spoke about being bullied. When I got placed in Tata, my parents were overjoyed. It wasn't what I wanted, but I went ahead with it anyways. That's where I fell in love for the first time. And, got my heart broken too. I was head over heels in love with a guy. I didn't know what was happening. So I told my best friend. She had a simple answer. 'Don't you know? You're gay.' And the next sentence made me who I am today. 'It's totally normal.' At home, relatives started asking about me. Unnecessary 'tips' about how my behaviour should be curbed were brushed aside by my mom.

Once during Diwali, I was making rangolis, when one of the relatives mentioned how my sister should do it instead. Man! That one was a two for two! My mom snapped back like the boss lady she is. That's the way it's always been—she's been a barrier between them and me all these years. When we were little, she sat my sister and me down and explained to us this one thing. 'Whatever you do, tell me everything. It's us against the world.' And, that's what encouraged me to come out to her when I was twenty-one. I broke down and I told her that I'd tried my best for twenty-one years. I just wasn't attracted to girls. I lay down in her lap, bawling my eyes out. She patted my head and said, 'that's all?'

I'm a celebrity hairstylist now. A long way from a kid working in Tata. I've embraced the part of me who loves art and culture and I'm even a nude model now. Yesterday, my mother was the first one who to text me congratulations after the verdict—it was as much her victory as it was mine. Since yesterday, she's going on about 'our future plans'—marriage, grandchildren, great grandchildren also—and I'm just like calm down, mom. One thing at a time!

SEEN IN
CHENNAI

SHE'S A MAHARASHTRIAN, and I'm a Gujarati. The first time I saw her was at a train station, and she was one of the most beautiful women I'd ever seen. But within minutes I lost sight of her—and didn't think I'd ever see her again. I worked at a factory near the station, and thought about her often—one of those days I spotted her again, at a shop on the opposite side. I realised she worked there, and for me it was a sign, but I was too shy to talk to her. After some time, when I finally had the courage and went up to her, she wasn't surprised at all! In fact, she told me that she noticed how I kept staring at her, and that I wanted to talk to her! I wanted to marry her right then, but she made me wait for six long years before we got together. She said that we're both from different castes, so unless her parents didn't agree, she wouldn't marry me. I knew I didn't want to be with anybody else, so even though I was scared, I decided to go talk to her parents. I told them that I didn't want to change anything about their daughter, I loved her for everything that she was, and wanted to spend my life with her. Somehow it worked, and they agreed!

Now it's been thirty-three long and wonderful years that we've spent together. We have four children, and all four of them have grown up knowing both our religions, languages, and cultures. And I made sure that happened—and that she never felt like she had to leave her roots or her identity behind, because at the end of the day we're equals. And I've always believed that if something as pure as true love brings you together, then no barrier like religion should be tearing you apart.

Nikon

IT'S NEVER TOO LATE TO PICK UP THE CAMERA AND YOU'RE NEVER TOO OLD TO GET BEHIND IT.

I **AM A BANKER BY PROFESSION**, but right from the day I touched a film camera and saw the Polaroids come out, I've been a photographer! I miss the roll camera days but I have now adapted to your DSLRs to explore more places and people.

In my many years of service at State Bank of India, one would often find me behind the lens rather than the cashier. A lot of my first exhibits were through the bank. My boss would let me off work early. I was the guy with a camera dangling around my shoulder. From capturing M.S. Subbulakshmi from the first row to working with dancers, icons and artists, I saw magic travel from B&W to colour. And it never ends. That small boy who ran around with the film camera still runs. So, when people call me the seventy-year old-photographer, I say 'It's never too late to pick up the camera and you're never too old to get behind it'.

And oh! All you millennials, for the love of God please stop looking up while fake-posing for pictures man; the heavens aren't calling you up that early!

I WAS IN MY THIRTIES WHEN I first met Marina—she had come to Jaisalmer all the way from Australia, for a desert safari. It was a five day trip and I taught her to ride a camel! These were the 1970s—*un dino, pehli nazar mein bhi pyaar ho jata tha*!

And that's exactly what happened—for both of us, it was love at first sight. Throughout the trip, we couldn't take our eyes off of each other. And before leaving for Australia, Marina said the three magical words to me—'I love you'. I turned red! Nobody had said those words to me before. I can never forget that day—I was feeling so shy that I couldn't utter a word in response to her confession!

But she understood and we stayed in touch. After Marina flew back, she'd write to me every week, and a few weeks later, she invited me to Australia—I was over the moon!

Without informing my family, I took a loan of Rs 30,000, bought a ticket to Melbourne, arranged for a visa and flew to be with her. Those 3 months were magical—she taught me English, and I taught her to do the ghoomar. But then she said, 'Let's get married and settle in Australia!' Things got complicated.

I wasn't ready to leave my motherland and she wasn't willing to move to India. I told her, 'This can't work long term,' and we decided to part ways. It wasn't easy—she cried a lot the day I left, but I had to let her go. Then, life moved on. A few years later, owing to family pressure, I had to get married. Afterwards, I took up a job as the gatekeeper of Kuldhara, the abandoned

AFTER, I TOOK UP A JOB AS THE GATEKEEPER OF KULDHARA, THE ABANDONED GHOST TOWN NEAR MY VILLAGE TO FEND FOR MY FAMILY.

ghost town near my village to fend for my family. But quite often, I'd find myself thinking about Marina. 'Would she have gotten married?', 'Will I ever see her again?' But I never had the courage to write to her. As time passed, memories faded. I got busy with family responsibilities. And then, two years ago, my wife passed away. All my sons were married and had moved out. And here I was, an eighty-two year-old man, gate keeping India's haunted village. And just when I thought that life couldn't surprise me anymore, it did! A month ago, out of nowhere, Marina wrote to me. She asked, 'How are you, my friend?' I got goosebumps. After fifty years, she'd found me! Since then, she's been calling me every day; we have so much to catch up on! She told me that she'd never gotten married and that she's coming to India soon. *Ramji ki kasam*, I feel like I'm twenty-one again! I don't know what the future holds, but knowing that my first love is back in my life and talks to me every day is a feeling I can't explain.

BERLIN TO BOMBAY, HOLOCAUST TO HAVEN

FROM BERLIN TO BOMBAY, my life has been anything but ordinary. For most of my childhood, my family and I were the 'Wandering Jews', on the run from Hitler. We lived in Berlin, had a beautiful apartment and Papa ran a successful company.

But as Hitler rose to power, Papa's company was taken away and we had to leave our home. Soon, Hitler began to round up us Jews, so when I was six years old, Papa called Mum and told her to pick me up from school and leave for Holland to see her parents. It was code for 'escape' but I was kept in the dark because of my loud mouth! Little did I know that it would be the last time I saw our home in Berlin—I was just glad to be done with school and see Oma and Oppa!

From Holland, we moved to Paris and for a few months, things were normal. I went to a nice school, picked up French, and spent my time collecting shells on the beach. But once again, the war caught up with us when World War II broke out.

Papa was taken away to an Assembly Camp, the whereabouts of which we didn't know. Ma and I were frantic—we didn't know if we would even see him again. The attacks escalated—air raids happened all the time and our only defence was a basement shelter two houses away, and a gas mask container, which my nine year-old self naively filled with candy!

One afternoon, the air raid sirens went off and we ran for shelter. There was an explosion—our house had been bombed, so we had to run again. The only silver lining was that we heard of where Papa was and decided to go look for him.

On the way, we evaded attacks, moved from town to town, and faced the German police machine-gunning intruders. We somehow managed to reunite with Papa and began planning our escape from Europe.

We had to get to Paris to get our Visa petitions, but at the border a German Gestapo stopped us. I thought that was the end of our lives, but Papa took advantage of our surname, which sounded German and pretended that we'd been on holiday. Thankfully, our passports didn't have a Jewish stamp and the Gestapo let us through. That night, Papa ordered the finest champagne to celebrate our new life. The Germans were behind us, but we were one step ahead.

When we got to Paris, our visa petitions were of no use—the US had closed all entry to Germans and we were stuck. So, we decided to seek refuge in Havana—a small Island that Papa chose because they had the best cigars! But they were only allowing Christians in, so overnight we 'changed' our religion on paper and forged baptism certificates to prove it. We had learnt to pretend by then.

After four long years, we boarded a ship to Havana. We were surrounded by Jewish refugees, but one oddly familiar voice kept calling out to Papa. He said, 'Fritz ... Fritz, don't you recognize me?' We turned around and didn't recognize the man. But then we saw a woman next to him, who was my aunt Olga and the man, unrecognizable because of how pale and weak he looked, was Papa's brother!

He'd just been released from a horrid concentration camp in exchange for German prisoners of war. We had lost most of our family to this war—my grandparents had been taken away by the Germans, and my relatives had either died in gas chambers or were nowhere to be found. So, to be reunited with my uncle and aunt felt surreal.

I celebrated my 11th birthday in Havana and spent the next four years there. Since we were always on the run, most of my friendships through the war were fleeting. But in Havana, I finally got to make some close friends—one of them was Florence. We were different in every way, but we really hit it off—she talked as much as I did and we became the best of friends! In fact, we both even had our first kiss with the same boy!

Sadly, we lost touch when we moved on to different places from Havana, but a couple of years ago, she put out an ad looking for me

in a paper read by German Jew Refugees. I saw the Ad and went to see her—we took one look at each other and fell into each other's arms, weeping.

But I think I've skipped too many decades, so let's get back to Havana in 1945. The war had ended and finally on our third attempt, we got our visa to the US. So, we flew to New York and celebrated my 15th birthday there. I thought it would be the last time I would have to shift bases, but as fate it would have it, the best move of my life was yet to come.

I met Anand on the dance floor. We were both studying at Wisconsin University and every other Friday my friends and I played music and taught foreign students western dance moves. But Anand always just sat in the corner. So once, I walked over to him and asked, 'Are you here to learn or what?', to which he replied, 'No no, I already know how to dance, I'm just here to see who's a good dancer—Will you dance with me?' And boy, was he a smooth dancer—just like my Papa! But it was going to take a lot more than a great dance for that 'goofball' to impress me!

That summer, Anand and I became friends and even went on double dates, but we were just one half of each couple. I would usually sit in the front of the car yakking away with my Egyptian friend, while he was getting friendly with an American girl in the back! But when our dates started liking each other, I wound up being stuck with Anand, but we were still just friends.

THROUGH EVERYTHING, ANAND WAS BY MY SIDE, REGARDLESS OF WHAT ANYONE SAID.

Then, as the harsh winter gave way to a beautiful spring morning, I decided to skip class to take a walk. And for reasons I still can't explain, my first call was to Anand, asking him to join me. We walked and talked about our hopes and dreams. By the time I came back to my room, I had fallen in love. Just as suddenly as spring had come, he had warmed his way into my heart.

We started dating as he took me around town and charmed me with his chivalry and wit—he was the kindest old soul I'd met. Life with him was great, until after a year, he suddenly called me up and told me that he had to go back to India—he couldn't marry a foreign girl and take her home to meet his Maharashtrian family! I still remember how miserable I felt when I saw him boarding that ship back to India—I thought I would never see him again.

But I had too much spirit to sit around and mope, so I called up my girlfriend, who had also just broken up with her Indian boyfriend, and said, 'Let's take a bachelor trip around Europe and have some fun!' We hopped through different cities, went for fancy dinners and parties, and had the time of our lives! Anand and I wrote letters to each other, but after that trip, I realized I needed to move on. I was sad when he wrote to me, and even sadder when he didn't. So, in a final letter to him, I said my goodbye, wished him a wonderful life and called it a day.'

Three weeks later, on an ordinary New York day, I received a phone call from Anand. He started incoherently mumbling French, a language he didn't speak, 'I want ... you should come here', I thought he'd gone bonkers or was very drunk, so I told him to write to me and hung up!

Two weeks later, when I opened my mail, I found an Indian Government Application letter from him applying for the position of being my 'husband' with all his qualifications listed. It said: 'Dear Madam, if the position of husband is still open, I would like to apply.'

I was certain he had gone totally mad so I asked an Indian friend who said, 'This is a proposal! He's asking to marry you, dammit!' My hands trembled as I called him back—I was so happy in that moment that I just started screaming 'yes' as soon as he answered!

But Papa said that he would have to come and ask for my hand. So, he came back just to meet my family. Papa spoke to him for several days which made me nervous, but secretly I knew he liked Anand—who wouldn't? Finally,

Papa agreed and we began discussing marriage.

Anand, being a dutiful Indian son, wanted to get married in Bombay, but Papa was firm and he said, 'She's not leaving New York until she's married'. So, we found the best of both worlds to keep our parents happy—a civil marriage in New York followed by a small ceremony in Bombay. I didn't want a big fat Indian wedding and there was no way I was doing the pheras—making the wife walk behind the husband wasn't my style!

After, Anand returned to India with the promise that I'd join him soon. He had to prepare his parents for the arrival of their new 'gori-gori' bride. I had been moving around my entire life, so I was excited—I even began learning Hindi! In a few weeks, I boarded a ship to India.

Forty-seven days later, I arrived at Bombay Port, wearing the only saree I owned, hoping to impress my in-laws, but I had obviously worn it all wrong! I still remember seeing Anand at the port—I was so excited. I waved to him and had my arms wide open for a hug, but he greeted me with a formal handshake. Confused, I shouted at him saying, 'I've come here to marry you dammit! Give me a hug!' and he whispered in return, 'Shh ... I can't, my uncle's right there looking at us!' and in my head I was like, 'Oh dear ... '

My first day in Bombay was ... noisy. The cars kept honking, and there were so many crows! But, the move to India felt a lot like Havana—the hot weather and 'kal karega' attitude was the same. Soon, I married Anand for the second time and we moved into a paying guest home, and started building our life.

Once we were settled in, I quickly realized that I wasn't the kitty party kind who could stay at home. I needed to work and be up and about. So, I did all kinds of things—I translated for German Journalists, interviewed celebrities for magazines, and even organised a couple of fashion shows!

I remember, in the beginning, my father-in-law was reserved about me—but never unkind. My mother-in-law on the other hand was thrilled that her son had brought home a 'gori' bride. Still, it wasn't an easy transition. Anand always said, 'Get their acceptance, then do what you want!' So, I took Marathi tuitions to talk to Ma, wore sarees and even let her call me by an Indian name—she picked 'Shanta Devi', but let me tell you, I was neither 'Shanta' nor a 'Devi!'

Eventually, I grew closer to my in-laws and would even tease Ma sometimes. Once, she asked me if I had chosen a saree to wear for a wedding and I said, 'No, but I just bought a pair of some really cool jeans, wanna see?' She stormed out of the room and I couldn't stop laughing!

But through everything, Anand was by my side, regardless of what anyone said. So, when we gave birth to two beautiful children, our different cultures never caused a conflict. We let the children be, refused to impose our own traditions onto them, and always acted as one unit. Our arguments would stay in the room and the kids couldn't play us against each other. In fact, when it came to picking names I told him, 'Hey, I chose the first one, so you get the other!' Today, we have a big family filled with kids and grandkids—Anand is Aja to them and I'm their Oma, which means grandmother in German. But just by the way, I speak fluent Hindi and Marathi!

Today, I'm eighty-nine years old, and sixty-four years of my life I've lived in this city—and

I'm not even Indian! But not once have I been made to feel like I didn't belong—it's a place where people smile back when you smile, and share a chapati with you even if they only have two. It's also the place where I raised my beautiful family with my husband—and that makes this home. Until three months ago, when I lost a piece of it ...

It's been a life well-lived with Anand. We traveled the world, listened to the same music, and found romance in the little moments—he'd send me flowers and I was always the first one to put my arms around him—ever since my first day in Bombay! A good evening to us was sitting at home and chatting away—even though I did most of the talking. He was so easy to be with—time flew by!

And in our sixty-four years together, we'd been married three different times; in New York, Bombay and once again on our 50th anniversary when we renewed our vows at the chapel next to City hall where we first got married! I always joked with him saying, 'Don't you ever divorce me, otherwise you'll have three alimonies to pay!' We joked like this all the time—he had a mischievous sense of humour that matched up to the cracks I took at him!

But our lifetime of banter came to an end six weeks before his 96th birthday—Anand passed away. He had been fading in and out for two years with only a few lucid moments and that's when I knew I was losing him. It was painful.

Old age had caught up with him and there came a point where there was nothing we could do to save him. I promised that I would never take him to the hospital a week before he died because what was the point of prolonging his pain? One of our last conversations, when he was barely lucid, went something like this—he was sitting on his chair, when I patted my hands on his thighs and said, 'Listen Buster, I've been married three times .... unfortunately all of them have been to the same man and still you never listen to me!' His one eye opened and he replied, 'Aapne badi galti ki'—those were his last words to me and I couldn't help but think—my God, he won the last round of jokes!

HE HAD BEEN FADING IN AND OUT FOR TWO YEARS WITH ONLY A FEW LUCID MOMENTS AND THAT'S WHEN I KNEW I WAS LOSING HIM. IT WAS PAINFUL.

It's been three months since and I spend my time doing the things I used to do with him—I watch plays, listen to music and visit friends for dinner whenever I can. I even drive on my own as long as there's guaranteed parking! I miss him every day, but I'd rather go out and take a swim than feel sorry for myself at home—I think Anand would be most shocked if that happened.

So here I am folks, eighty-nine, putting on some make up and showing up every day ... I have a life to live for two people now, so I'm busy making the most of it!

I WAS THE ONLY FEMALE FIELD AGENT IN THE ENTIRE COMPANY, AND COULDN'T UNDERSTAND WHY.

A**KRITI, GO FIND OUT WHO** that guy is dating?', 'Akriti, find out if she likes me?'—you can tell, I was an investigator since my school days, but never in my wildest dreams did I think I'd become a detective. I'd just finished my MBA and saw an ad in the paper asking for detectives. I had nothing to lose, so I applied. When I went into my interview, there was hesitancy on both sides. I didn't know what I was getting myself into and the man interviewing me kept asking if I was sure I wanted to apply for this position. I was surprised when I was offered the job but I immediately accepted. I was the only female field agent in the entire company. I loved what I did, but of the 100 suggestions I made to my boss, he'd maybe accept one! I was tired of constantly having to prove my worth, so at twenty-four I took the leap of faith and started my own Detective Agency. I had roadblocks constantly, from trying to get a loan to start the business, to recruiting for it! But I kept trying until I managed to get the loan and found a team that did.

My first case was a pre-marriage check and since then, we've grown to solve all kinds of cases.

But there have always been challenges; after all, we live in a man's world. Just two hours ago I got off the phone with a man who couldn't understand how I, a woman, was going to solve his case—he wanted to talk to a man!

But, sometimes you just need to let your work do the talking—today, I have a team of over ninety-five detectives, with branches all over the country and we solve almost 100 cases per month! I've solved complex cases involving politicians and businessmen and have donned all kinds of disguises—from a chaiwali to a college girl!

I know I'm a woman who isn't working an expected normal white-collar job, but I haven't let that stop me. There are always going to be people out there who don't believe that a woman can stand on her own two feet and create something of her own. I'm here to tell you that she can!

I WASN'T BORN IN A WELL TO DO family. Dad worked an outstation job and made a meagre salary that couldn't support my seven siblings and mom. On weekends my siblings and I went to weddings hoping to receive half a coconut or fruit. I went to an English school, but I knew I had to start earning, so after the 10th Grade, I dropped out. I travelled North and took up odd jobs, until I was hired as a typist for Rs 30 a month—most of which I sent back home.

A few months later, my brother and I saw a recruitment Ad for the army and decided to apply. After forty-five tests and interviews—I was selected! That was the first time I actually 'celebrated'.

My training was rigorous—but I refused to give up. I worked on myself and became capable. Then, I went back to my family for two months and learnt that my parents had started finding partners for me. My relatives set me up with my now-wife. We barely knew each other—but over time, we fell in love and built a life.

In 1947, when partition was declared, a bloodbath ensued and my academy was responsible for protecting civilians. The operation lasted until September 1947—it had been tough, emotionally and physically. I used to train with Muslim candidates who were transferred to the newly formed Pakistan Army. We arranged a farewell party and said our final goodbyes.

Eventually, life moved on ... In 1963, I got a posting in London—we had a son by then and my wife was glad we could educate him there. My kids eventually graduated and I decided to retire from my duty. We came back to India and began leading a happy life. After forty-nine years together, my wife bid farewell to the world.

That was the turning point in my life—I began introspecting. I started practicing yoga, meditated and kept up with my exercise. I was visiting my son when I learnt that he had finished the Marine Corp Marathon. This awakened the old spirit in me and I decided to run the marathon!

I was eighty-four then and my son trained me for six weeks. In 2010 I ran my first marathon and won the first prize. Since then, I've run it every year. But the most memorable one is the 2016 marathon—at the age of ninety, I was the oldest participant.

It was raining, but I kept pushing myself—when the path became steeper, my son asked me to stop. I couldn't—I hadn't given up while facing the enemy's bullets during the Indo-China War, or when I was asked to swim without knowing how. My mind finally won over my body and I finished that thirteen-mile marathon, to loud cheers and a tight hug from my son.

That's how I've lived my life—through everything, I've just simply not given up. The art of being stubborn has helped me deal with some of the toughest times. I will participate in more marathons—I refuse to quit; I've got one life, and I can't waste it. I want to keep running; flying even—because this life, this time, is all we've got and we can't take it for granted!

BOTH MY PARENTS ARE DEAF AND MUTE, so I was raised by my grandparents; I hear stories about my childhood from them. When I was two days old, I was at the edge of the bed and about to fall. I wept for several minutes; obviously my parents couldn't hear me. My grandma finally heard, came in and took me to her bedroom. From that day, I slept in my grandparents room every night.

As I grew older, my parents and I barely communicated. I used gestures and lip read, but only when it was necessary. I'd show them my grades and ate with them—that was the only time we spent together. I'd see my friend's dads taking them out on motorbike rides. I'd ask nani, 'Baba can never take me out like this right?' After school, I'd want to tell them all about what I did, the friends I made, the boys I liked. I wanted to tell them about the insecurities I had with my own body. I wanted to vent to them when my crush rejected me, when kids made fun of my height and weight and called me nati and sukhri.

Some kids would even mock my parents. One kid said, 'Your father can't even hear , so what can he do?' I broke down. My teacher noticed and took him to the principal's office. I felt lost. I'd cry quietly after I got home, but I didn't let them see it. It broke me to see dad getting rejected from jobs and mom not having any friends or people to talk to. My dad worked as a data entry operator for twenty-one years. It was a typing job, but when the job required him to make calls, he was fired. I'd see him spend all his time googling, 'Jobs to help deaf people earn for their family'. Mom was a painter with an association for deaf and mute people for a few years, but she left her job because she had OCD.

I DECIDED TO LEARN SIGN LANGUAGE AND INTERNED WITH A SCHOOL FOR DEAF AND MUTE KIDS FOR A MONTH.

After that, we were living on my grandpa's pensions and savings. With every passing day, I ached to know what my parents were going through. So after 12th grade, I decided to learn sign language and interned with a school for deaf and mute kids for a month, and then started taking private tuitions for them alongside college. I did this for five years; every minute I spent with a child made me realise how tough life was for my parents. The kids required long hours and a lot of patience, but I needed to do this.

After college, I began applying for jobs aggressively and got accepted as a client servicing manager at Wipro. It's better for us financially, but my parents don't know sign language, so we still communicate using gestures ... I finally understand what they're going through. I get very upset when I think of their frustration, but if they catch me crying they get so anxious. They try asking me what's wrong using hand gestures, but I never tell them—I don't want them to worry. I make silly excuses, and try to make them smile. The only thing that matters to me is their happiness and I want to spend all my time making them realise that they're being looked after; that they're so loved.

THIS HOUSE WAS BUILT BEFORE MY GRANDFATHER'S TIME—it's more than 150 years old! We've always lived in a joint family so my entire childhood was spent playing around here with my brothers. We used to have a ration shop in those days, but during a flood in 1961, everything was destroyed. Our house was damaged and we even lost two truckloads of our stock. Since we were running our shop from home, we lost our roof and our livelihood, all in one day. It was a really bad time, but we knew one thing—we brothers had to stick together for our family, for our ancestral home.

So, we took bank loans and worked hard to return the house to its former glory. My entire family of more than twenty people stuck together—we were there for each other and together, we built ourselves from the ground up. It took us almost twenty-five years to completely recover from that incident. But it taught me one thing—that a 'house' is just bricks and mortar at the end of the day. The only reason we did what we did to restore that house was because of my brothers and my family—for our home.

WHY ARE YOU ASKING ME SO MANY SERIOUS QUESTIONS? LEAVE ALL THAT AND COME DANCE WITH ME!

SEEN IN
VARANASI

I STARTED DRESSING UP LIKE GANDHIJI for my grandkids initially. I would teach them good things like honesty, fighting for what you believe in ... They started applying what I told them in their lives and it made me really happy. That's when I realized that other people would listen to me too because of my resemblance to Bapu. So now I travel to different cities around his birthday every year to talk about important issues. I love looking like the man who's inspired me all my life—and if I can do some Gandhi-giri along the way, why not?

TRIGGER WARNING: I was born and brought up in a chawl. While growing up, both my parents would constantly fight with each other, my dad even had an alleged 'partnership' with a lady and that deeply disturbed my mom. The fights got so bad that my father refused to contribute at home, and once even beat my mother black and blue with a belt.

When my mother got really tired of everything, she took me to the beach, to drown both me and herself in the sea. But in that moment, she realised that quitting wasn't an option, she needed to take a stand for herself.

A few days after that, when there was another fight, my mother filed a police complaint against my father. But after some questioning, they sent him back home.

We spent a few years like that, where my dad would keep tormenting us, while my mother would threaten to complain to the police. Soon I joined college, and that's when I met someone I fell madly in love with. He was five years older than me. He became my anchor, and I got attached to him very quickly. Then he suddenly told me he didn't want to be with me anymore.

I was heartbroken. On the same day, my father and I too had a big fight. I was so exhausted of all the emotional trauma, that I decided to end my life. I went to a nearby street, stood there and drank a whole bottle of phenyl.

The next thing I remember is waking up in a hospital bed. I'd been in the ICU for four days. My dad visited me and told me if I really wanted to commit suicide, 'I should've researched better'. I got out within one week, and realised I'd lost

THE SCARS OF MY PAST ARE STILL FRESH AND STILL BOTHER ME FROM TIME TO TIME.

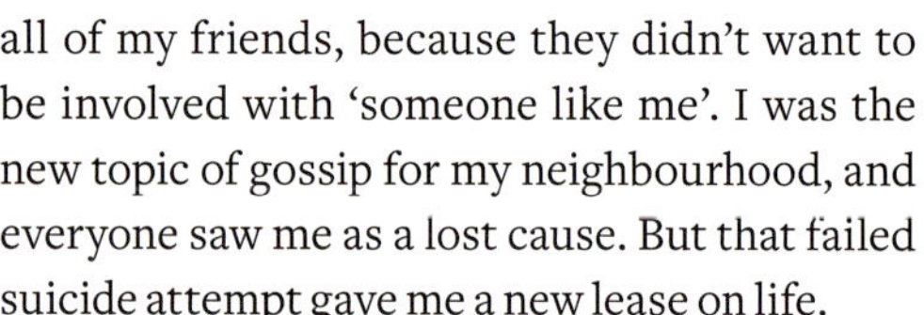

all of my friends, because they didn't want to be involved with 'someone like me'. I was the new topic of gossip for my neighbourhood, and everyone saw me as a lost cause. But that failed suicide attempt gave me a new lease on life.

I was asked to go for counselling, and was even given medication to help me get myself together. That changed my perspective on how I viewed my life. Soon, my mom and I moved out and got ourselves a house.

I embraced my past and realised that I had nothing to be ashamed of. I pursued a Masters in Journalism, and after that got a job with All India Radio. It's been a few years now, and I'm in a much better place in life.

I've even opened my own organisation where on different occasions, me and a few other people go out and serve tea to the police officers on duty. Of course, the scars of my past are still fresh and still bother me from time to time. So, what I'm really trying to say is before judging someone the next time, or stereotyping them in a certain way, remember that everyone, everywhere is going through something and a little bit of kindness from you could be the difference between life and death.

MY MOTHER GOT ME MARRIED at the age of sixteen, to someone who was twenty-six years old. And within four months of the marriage, I was pregnant. My in-laws wouldn't let me study, and they'd treat me like I was their servant. Once, when I was eight months pregnant, there was a theft in the house and my in-laws blamed me. They starved and tortured me till I had to beg for them to stop.

I got so sick after that that I started vomiting blood. So, I packed my bags and went to my mother's house. My husband came along, to take care of me and our child. Soon, I gave birth. My husband was working as a driver but we realised that his income wasn't enough. So, I took up a job as well. I was still a minor, so the only job I got was as a teacher's assistant, with a pay of Rs 2000 a month.

One day, suddenly, my husband said he wasn't comfortable with me working. But I wanted to continue to earn for my child. So a few days later, he decided to move back with his parents, and soon I got a letter saying that he had remarried. I was left alone with a two year-old child at the age of eighteen. I needed to earn more and I knew there was no way I could do it without any qualifications. So I decided to take my mother's help and finish my 12th grade. I continued to work to sustain the house. And when I finally finished 12th grade, I got a job at a media company. I knew I had the potential to do more, but the fact that I didn't have a degree held me back. Both my mom and I had run out of money, and had no savings left. I was at a dead end, and worried that I wouldn't be able to give my son the life he deserves.

One of those days, my boss sensed that something was wrong with me. She called me and asked me what had happened, I couldn't control myself and told her everything. She asked me not to worry. And just a few days later, she handed me an envelope of Rs 15000, and said, 'This is yours to use, go for it and don't ever look back'.

MY SON AND I LOVE EACH OTHER TO BITS, AND WE BOTH KNOW THAT WE'RE ENOUGH FOR EACH OTHER.

That was my turning point. I finished my bachelors and even managed to get a great job as a project manager afterwards. Today, I'm twenty-three and running my house single-handedly. I'm paying for my son's education and saving up to secure his future.

My husband refuses to give me a divorce till I don't give 'his son' back to him. He refuses to help us or even check up on us. But I'm okay with it, I've cried, stumbled and fallen but I'm standing on my own two feet now. My son and I love each other to bits, and we both know that we're enough for each other. It's us against the world, and if we've made it this far, we'll make it to the end.

I MET MY HUSBAND WHEN I WAS TWENTY. We fell in love and got married by the age of twenty-three. We had a good twenty years together, but we grew apart. At the age of forty-seven, we got a divorce. Both my kids were abroad, so I started my life anew. I'd never signed a cheque, let alone live by myself. But I was eager to figure it out.

My friend called me about an opening at her school; after the interview, I had a job! Every day I'd work, I'd take tuitions and go to the gym. I had a fire within me to live again!

I had a new dream—my own house. I had my eye on this beautiful apartment with a great view of the skyline! With my savings, alimony and a loan from my sister, I got my very own home! It was in shambles, but I was ready to do the work. I bought a mattress to sleep on and bit by bit, it became a home.

Four years later, one of my friends signed me up on a home stay service. I was ready to try new things—so, why not? I began hosting people from all over the world! I guess my home was magic, because every person left happy. A man we hosted invited us for his wedding! I even became financially independent.

The happiest moment by far was when I saved enough to book a vacation for my daughter and I abroad! Since then, I plan one trip with her every year. The world has opened up for me! But no view in the world is better than the one from my window. It reminds me of something I built on my own. And I know that life always gives you a second chance and miracles happen when you least expect them.

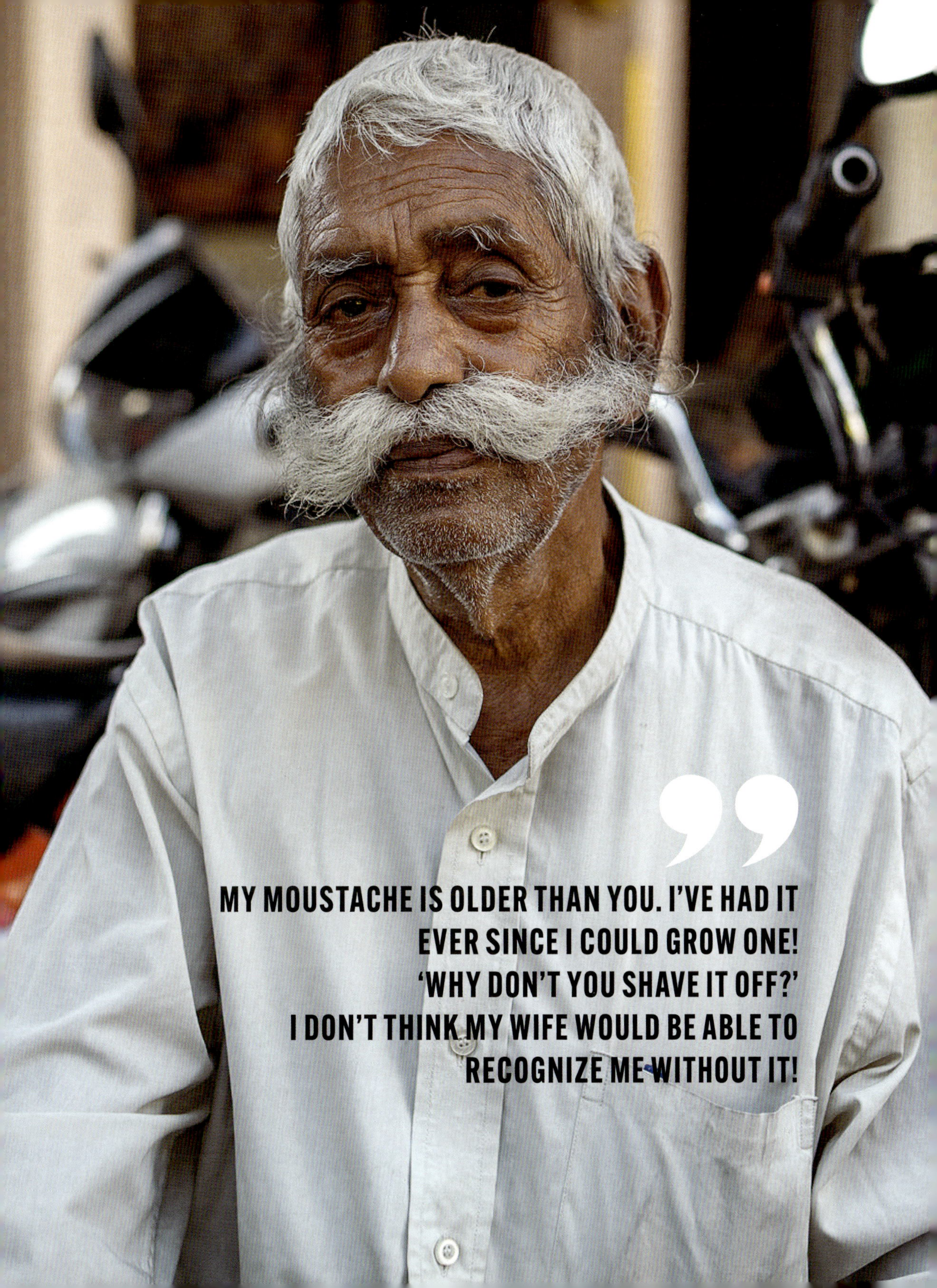

MY MOUSTACHE IS OLDER THAN YOU. I'VE HAD IT
EVER SINCE I COULD GROW ONE!
'WHY DON'T YOU SHAVE IT OFF?'
I DON'T THINK MY WIFE WOULD BE ABLE TO
RECOGNIZE ME WITHOUT IT!

I'D BEEN WORKING AS A FISHERMAN FOR THE LAST TWENTY YEARS, But because of bad weather and it being so risky out there in the sea—we aren't allowed to fish for now. But I still have to earn—so I work as a garbage collector here. I don't really enjoy this job and sometimes I get really tired—because no matter how much I clean, the littering never stops. But there's nothing I can do, I have to keep going—to be able to put food on the table for my family. And the only thought that's keeping me happy right now is my wife—knowing that she'll be lovingly cooking for me and waiting for me to get home soon so we can eat dinner together! I have to get back to work now, but if you want to write something about my story, write this— the next time you want to throw something out of the window, think of me with this big garbage bag, picking up litter all day ... and don't!

I WON'T EVER FORGET THAT DAY—9 February 2014. I was in my third year of college. My househelp hadn't shown up, so I was cleaning my art studio. I sketched for some time and then left to meet my friends. I'd almost arrived, when I got a call from my neighbour; a feeling of dread settled in my chest.; She said, 'Amrai, there's smoke coming out of your place!' I rushed back—We tried calling for the fire brigade, but the local fire station wasn't operational that day. We finally got the door opened; all I could see was darkness. When I went inside, I saw that the only space that was ruined was my studio. It had my entire life's work in there and my submissions were due in a month! But by some miracle, the closet that held my certificates remained untouched. I was numb that night. But the next day, my mother said something that changed my perception. She told me my hands were fine and I could create everything again.

So that's what I did—I achieved in one month, what normally takes a year! I got consumed in my art. I managed to top my batch, despite everything! The fire within me turned out to be greater than the fire around me. I guess, all my art really needed was a 'spark'.

WHEN I WAS twelve, I got electrocuted while playing and had to get my right arm amputated—I underwent over forty surgeries on both my arms. It hindered everything, from writing to wearing my uniform, to just walking outside. No outing was complete without strangers staring at me.

Luckily, over time, I started doing things on my own and felt more confident about my arm. And at twenty-five, I married my college sweetheart, who never saw it as a hindrance. Five years later, we had our daughter, Meher. It was the happiest day of my life. But over the next three months, my life changed completely. I could barely hold Meher—someone always had to hand her to me. I couldn't change her diaper, and I wasn't even producing enough milk to feed her. I felt like a bad mother—I failed to do the most basic things for my baby.

THE ONE THING THAT REMAINS CONSTANT IS THE LOVE.

Even my body changed. I had saggy breasts, a belly bulge and gained ten kgs. I felt ugly and irritable.

I stayed up all night having meltdowns. I'd snap easily and had ugly fights with my husband and mom. I'd often tell them that they didn't understand what I was going through. All I could think about was life never being the same again. I knew I was experiencing postpartum depression, even though I wasn't diagnosed. Things started getting better two months later. Meher grew bigger, so I felt more confident about holding her. I even started trying to change her diaper. To cope with the stress, I started new shows and went on drives with my husband and friends in the evenings after Meher slept. But I'm still not a 100 per cent there with being able to care for Meher on my own. I'm still not able to bathe her. Yesterday I was home alone with her, and it took me five attempts to change her diaper. Even after that, it wasn't on her right. But I'm setting small goals for myself every day, and getting there slowly.

It's been seven months, and I still get mood swings, but Meher's coos and grunts lift my spirits—she's always smiling! I'm looking for the small wins, the little things to look forward to—like right now, my husband and I are planning a holiday with Meher hopefully next year. I can't wait for sunny beach days with our baby—the first as a family! Motherhood is beautiful, no doubt, but it isn't always rosy. Our bodies change; our lives change. But the one thing that remains constant is the love—and that always pulls us through.

I'VE ALWAYS FELT STRONGLY about determining my own future. I was only sixteen when I told my parents that I wanted to be a psychologist. All they asked of me was to be sure that that's what I wanted to do for the rest of my life. I was sure.

So, after I graduated from a college in the USA, my father advised me to not come back to India because psychology isn't valued that much here. But I knew I wanted to change some of the issues the people in our country face—the restrictions, the unnecessary social norms, the shame a rape survivor has to suffer. I wanted to make a difference at home. After coming back, I began practicing—I wasn't making too much progress, but I was happy. At least I thought it was—until one morning, I woke up to the news of the Nirbhaya rape case. I'm the daughter of an army man and I was taught to never fear anything or anyone. But for the first time in my life, I was afraid to even travel by myself ... I was actually afraid for my life. I'd worked with several rape victims before, but I'd never seen anything so brutal. I was on the verge of losing my trust in humanity—and so that I didn't lose it completely, I decided to do something about it. I started an NGO for the victims of rape and abuse. We have a 24/7 helpline. Imagine this—a woman is raped and she calls a number for help, but they tell her to call back at 9 a.m.

WE'RE TRYING TO BREAK THE CYCLE OF HELPLESSNESS AND EMPOWER WOMEN TO STAND UP FOR THEMSELVES.

How ridiculous is that? So now, we direct the police, social workers or hospitals to the location of where these women call from, no matter the time of the call. But we can't make much of a difference unless we tackle the actual problem—mindsets. Not just of men, but also of women. We're trying to break the cycle of helplessness and empower women to stand up for themselves. Unfortunately, at the end of the day, there is a prevalent rape culture here and it's not a problem that can be solved overnight. But we're getting there with the help of progressive minds like that of my father. He always says, 'I'm not raising you to be independent like a man, I'm raising you to be independent like a human!' And that's what we're really trying to achieve. To see women as humans whose birth right is just ... equality.'

WHEN I WAS YOUNGER, I used to see these men wearing pants and shirts and think they were really respected, well-dressed men. So, I moved out of my village to find a respectable job. My parents were uneducated, but taught me one thing, 'struggle, but don't cheat.' With that principle, I came to the city. I worked in a hotel first—washing dishes, serving and cleaning the floor. My salary was only Rs 50. From there, I worked at people's homes with imaandari. Once my employer taught me how to make pizzas. I caught on easily. Eventually I realised I needed to do something more ... So, I left and opened up my own small stall. Some days I didn't make much money. But thankfully, people liked my food! That kept me going. And in a few years, I saved enough money to open a restaurant.

It was also my dream to buy a house. Once, when I asked a flat owner if I could buy a house in his building ... he told me that I won't be able to afford it. I told him not to judge me by the way I look. And with my first big saving, I became the owner of a new house. And when the man I spoke to welcomed me, he said, 'This building is open to anyone who wants to live here'—he was done judging a book by it's cover. The restaurant kept getting bigger and bigger. I paid off my loans—I still don't know how to read and write but I educated my children. Now, forty years later—I'm the owner of a jewellery shop, an imitation store and Ramu's Open House! But what people don't know is—when we're short staffed, I'm a server here too. I will never forget my roots.

WHAT DO YOU WANT TO BE WHEN YOU GREW UP? I HAVE NEVER REALLY GIVEN IT MUCH THOUGHT. I'VE ALWAYS BEEN SURE OF ONE THING THOUGH. I DON'T WANT TO BE JUST A 'WIFE'.

I WAS BUYING FOOD FROM a roadside stall when I was tapped on the shoulder by a lady with a howling child in her arms. When I offered her money, she said she needed food and asked me to buy it for her. I think this had to do with trust. In a way, I think she wanted me to know that I could trust that she was using the money for something useful. After buying her some dal and rice, I realized we were both walking back in the same direction, towards my house. Being the curious person that I am, I asked her where she lived. I was so surprised when she pointed out to the footpath that I walked past every day on my way to work. I had never noticed her or her family before. And even if I had, I had normalized it and never actually paid attention. But I paid attention now—I saw the Kharwar family, the children sleeping on rags, mosquitoes flying all around them, and a sheet that covered their 'house'. I, on the other hand, lived in a good building with a roof and security—I had the ability to do something. I sent out a message on a WhatsApp group and in a day, I received a mattress, children's clothes, and envelopes of money. And in fifteen days I had Rs 50,000!

It's really amazing what one call for help can do. In no time, the Kharwar family moved into a house in Worli, paying Rs 4000 in monthly rent. It's a small house but they have a roof over their heads and they are surrounded by other families and children. I became very close to them. Since I lost my grandmother a few weeks ago, they have checked up on me at least twice a week and always offer to bring me food. We've really become a family. In fact, they even asked me to name their son! I realized that I was able to bring people together from all over to change the destiny of a whole family; if I could do it for one family, I could do it for others too. Since then, with the help of fundraising and sending out messages to friends and family, I've raised Rs 44,000 for another family.

My goal is to rehabilitate them before the end of the year so they have a positive start to their new year. I think that if we have the power in our lives to destroy one's struggles, be it humans or animals, we should do it. What good comes from sitting on our own, with all our successes and wealth, when the world around us is suffering?

EVER SINCE I WAS BORN, my mom has had to face unsolicited advice. I'm dark-skinned, so distant relatives would give her tips on how to make me 'fairer'. My mom never bothered about it, and brushed it off when it became a topic of conversation. It got worse when my brother was born. He was fairer than me. Endless comparisons poured in. Even at school I was compared to a crow. Everyone around me would carry on about being 'fair' and the cosmetics they'd use to achieve it. Through all of this, it was deeply engraved in my mind, that my skin colour wasn't normal. That affected how I felt about myself and my life. I was disturbed and would think about it all the time. My mom even suggested that I get therapy. I hit my lowest point when I wanted to play the lead in a school play. I was meant for it. But, I was asked to play the role of a tree instead since it would 'match my skin colour'. That day, I cried for hours. After that, I decided to quit theatre and join sports. Being out there in the sun would at least give me an excuse for why I was 'dark'. Even when I'd go out of the house, I'd always cover my face. But one day, I was out with a friend and my hands were over my face. My friend saw that, and suddenly swatted my hands off. She looked me straight in the eye and told me that I was gorgeous. She said that my skin was my identity and the most beautiful colour she'd seen! It was the first time that I received a compliment. It was a wake-up call for me.

I WAS ASKED TO PLAY THE ROLE OF A TREE INSTEAD SINCE IT WOULD 'MATCH MY SKIN COLOUR'.

For too long, I had let other people's opinions affect the way I felt. More than anything else, I had let one small thing take control of my entire identity. It was tough, but I made small changes every day. I stopped covering my face, applying layers of sunscreen and drowned the sound of haters. Once I went on a date with a guy, who told me 'You're pretty for a dark-skinned girl'. I just got up and left. I learned to value and appreciate myself. And can I tell you one thing? When I started doing that, it felt like the universe was now in my favour. People started loving my confidence, opportunities opened up and life didn't seem unfair anymore. I guess sometimes it just takes a strong belief in yourself, and seeing yourself as perfect just the way you are, for the world to fall in love with you too. To not doubt yourself, or think that you're lacking in some way, but to know that you're brave and beautiful and that a frivolous standard of beauty has got nothing on you.

PATRIARCHY≠POWER

I BELONG TO AN ORTHODOX MUSLIM FAMILY IN MUKKAM, KERALA; ONE WHERE GIRLS AREN'T MEANT TO HAVE A VOICE, AND MOST DAYS, AREN'T EVEN SUPPOSED TO EXIST.

That's why my biological father left my mom when he found out she'd given birth to me, a girl. She remarried soon after—I lived with my mom, stepfather and four stepsiblings.

My days were all the same—I'd go to school and do household chores after; I didn't have many friends. But there was a certain lifestyle that had to be followed, where men made all the decisions. They'd even eat before us—we were to serve them while they ate. For me, this was normal; it was all I knew.

One day, when I got back home from school, there were two people sitting in the veranda. My mom asked me to serve them tea—I did as I was told. I remember, I was still in my uniform. They smiled when I served them and left soon after. That's when mom said they'd come to see me—I was to be married to the boy.

I was shocked—I wasn't expecting it. Moreover, I knew there was something different about him. By chance, we'd studied autism that day and he ticked all the boxes. But my mom simply wrote it off saying he was shy. To her, it was enough he had all his limbs, no crooked teeth and didn't drink—what more could a girl want? But I was freaking out—I did not want to get married. For the first time in my life, I said,

'No' in a tone I'd never used before. But it fell on deaf ears—they fixed my marriage to him. I cried, pleaded and stayed hungry. All the while, mom's emotional blackmail continued; she threatened to commit suicide.

Apparently, calling off the wedding would bring 'shame' to the family as my sisters were yet to be married. My last resort was to talk to my to-be-husband. I called and begged him to call it off. His only reply was, 'What are you wearing right now?' I was at a loss for words—I had no out.

What's worse is that during the Nikaah, you don't even need the bride to be present—my father could just 'hand me over' to the groom. Which is what happened. I'd been eighteen for just three days. No one bothered to ask me what I wanted, what I thought—my fate was written without my consent and at eighteen I was bound to a man I didn't know.

On the night of the wedding, when he reached out to touch me, I lost it. I remember running circles around the bed trying to get away from him, screaming and crying. I couldn't calm down, so my mother-in-law made me sleep in her room. My father was called the next day, and I was sent back home. I was glad—I preferred death over being forced to bed with someone I didn't know.

Once again, my mom threatened to commit suicide as I'd shamed the family. But I wouldn't go back, no matter what. I told my mother that instead of her, I'd commit suicide—then there'd be no shame,

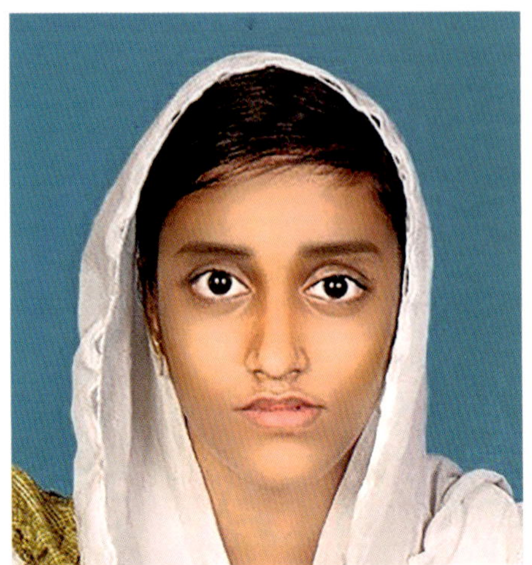

right? My parents asked me to not take any steps till my younger sisters got married. I didn't want them to suffer because of me, so I kept quiet for one whole year. Throughout, I knew they thought I was a burden.

But once they were settled in their lives, I asked for a divorce. My parents knew it was coming. They couldn't even refute me, because somewhere they understood they'd made a mistake. The village presidents were called to sit for the divorce proceedings. The patriarchy ran so deep that I wasn't even allowed to sit there—I was made to sit in another room, while the men discussed my marriage.

But I could hear them. When my parents brought up the fact that they'd hidden that the guy was autistic, the village presidents blamed my parents—because they didn't bother to find out or crosscheck anything, this was on them. How was that fair? I remained silent.

But when someone said, 'In Islam, if your husband wants to have sex with you, you can't say no. If you do, you're the lowest of the low', I came out of the room. I confronted the man who was representing my husband. I asked him if he had any daughters and if he did, what would he have done for them if they were in the same situation.

Everyone was stunned into silence—no one expected me, a girl, to speak up. The only response I got was, 'What's happened has happened. If your husband got paralyzed after marriage, would you leave him?' When I think about it now, I know it was the shittiest example they could've used.

Since I refused to give in, with no other choice, the divorce was finalized after that meeting. 'Talaq, talaq, talaq,' was written down on a piece of paper and that was the end of it. I lost my freedom with three words, and I found my freedom once again with just three words.

But my freedom was short lived—I was back home where every day felt like a battle. Without my family's support, I was unable to complete my education. But I wanted to be self-sufficient, so every day, I'd say, 'I want to work, I want to work,' almost as if I was chanting a mantra. After a point, they had no choice but to let me work.

I applied to be an executive at a vehicle showroom and got the job. I was always meek, but there I had to speak up and convince people to buy scooters. It helped boost my confidence—at work, and at home. But society thought it was their birth right to constantly remind me that I was a divorcee.

On the bus, people would stare at me, whisper behind my back and sometimes taunt me to my face—they'd say, 'Oh, he divorced you!' At first, I felt ashamed and would try to hide if I saw anyone who knew me. But then, I was just pissed off—why should I have to hide? So, the next time someone taunted me, I said, 'He didn't divorce me, I divorced him!'

Soon enough, the pressure mounting at home reached an all time high as the question arose, 'When will you get married?' I remember, my family would send people to see me at my office—without informing me! It was the same drama all over again—according to them, I had to somehow shun this label of being a 'divorcee'.

It's not like I wasn't open to the idea of marriage; I was. But I had one condition: I insisted on talking to the guy before I said yes. I began meeting guys, but either I rejected them or I was rejected for being too straightforward; I told everyone of my past with no shame. This continued for a while until one day, a well-built guy came to see me.

When I spoke to him, I told him the truth. He was broadminded—in fact when I told him that I was still a virgin, he said that it didn't matter. It was almost unbelievable that such a guy existed in our community. I liked him and agreed to the alliance.

I happily attended my Nikaah—I was head over heels for him. On the wedding night, I waited for him, bubbling with anticipation. When he entered the room, before I could even react, he slapped me and I fell to the floor. When I gathered my wits and asked him why he slapped me, he pulled me by my hair and said, 'What else do you expect? You're second-hand.'

'Second-hand.' All it took was one word to shatter my trust in him. I was so shocked that my brain went numb and I began sobbing. I was so traumatized, that I didn't even realize when he tied my hands and legs to the bed. He then brutally raped me—the pain was unimaginable. When I woke up the next day, he behaved as if nothing had happened; I convinced myself that it was normal.

I'd left my job before the wedding, because I was expected to be a loving housewife, who'd cook and clean. I had to learn to deal with my situation—I couldn't be a two-time divorcee. But I got another blow—I found out that my husband was a drug addict. To his family, he was the perfect son, but behind closed doors he'd get high on crystal meth. He was smart—he didn't indulge in alcohol because he knew people would be able to smell it on him.

I was the only one who was subjected to his evil side. On our 'honeymoon', I even caught him having sex with his someone else. I lost all hope as the abuse continued—he loved to see people in pain. I lost weight and would always have bruises all over my body. Whenever I visited my parents, I'd wear full sleeves—we had to play the part of the perfect couple for society. Once, when my sister saw a bruise on my neck, I lied to her and said that I had a fall.

My family thought I was happy. All the while, he'd constantly threaten to kill me, to chop me up into pieces or even fake my suicide. He had a good reputation, so even if I told anyone, no one would believe me. I was terrified, and began recording the abuse on my phone as evidence. What if I died and no one knew what really happened to me? I gave my cousin the password to my phone.

For three months, he tied me up and raped me. I was very naive back then—because when I found out I was pregnant, I thought he'd change. How wrong was I; when I told him, he kicked me in the stomach. I cried out loud and he tried to cover my mouth to silence me. But when I started bleeding, he had no choice but to take me to the hospital. We were on our way there, when he tried to kill me.

We were on his scooter when he threw me off it, hoping I'd get hit by a car. I survived but instead of taking me to the hospital, he took me to his sister's house. She was shocked at my state and forced him to take me to the hospital. There, I was able to call my mother. I was bleeding when the doctor said that I had an ectopic pregnancy, and if I didn't have surgery immediately, I'd die. Hearing this, my husband decided to waste six hours fighting with the doctor; he hoped time would do its job and I'd bleed out.

That's when my mom got suspicious and pushed to get the operation done—but I'd lost my baby. The next day, he called my mother and asked for a divorce—he said that I was disrespectful towards his parents, and that I refused to have sex with him. Which was ridiculous—I was pregnant for God's sake! He knew what had happened in my first marriage, and cunningly used the same reason.

Again, my mom blamed me—that's when I told her the truth. I even told her that I'd go back to him, to save my family from shame. But she said, 'You won't go back'. I was furious—he'd killed my child. So even though my wound hadn't healed and I could barely walk, I began going to the police station to get an FIR filed against him; but no one cared.

One day, my mom and I went to his house to get my gold and certificates back—but he kicked my stomach again and even slapped my mom. I was rushed to the hospital and finally, the police had no choice but to take my statement. They couldn't immediately register my case, but he was arrested for slapping my mother and was taken into remand for fourteen days. By the time he got out on bail, my FIR was filed.

He knew that there was no way he could avoid going to jail, so he tried to settle outside of court. But I was fuming—I refused to let that man roam free. He kept skipping court dates, while I waited for hours in court. While I was there, I began talking to other Muslim women who were fighting similar cases—most of them were waiting for a resolution for over five years.

Is that what I wanted my life to become? I was twenty—I had a lifetime ahead of me. Why should I suffer more because of him? I had to accept that it would take too long for him to be sentenced, but I could build a better future for myself. I made a deal with him—I'd withdraw my case if he gave back my gold and certificates, and sign the divorce papers. He agreed; I silenced my anger and moved on.

But I was done—with the judicial system, with Kerala, with India. I wanted to go somewhere no one knew me; I wanted to live peacefully. But once again, my family stood in my way. They wanted to keep me at home and to make sure I didn't leave the country or get a job, they burned my passport and certificates.

I was desperate—I turned against my parents. I filed a complaint against them in the Women's Cell for burning my documents, and not letting me leave. I tried everything—I told my mother that I'd publicly shame her; that I'd go to the media. They agreed to get new documents organized if I signed an agreement stating that I had no right to the family property.

I just wanted to leave, and agreed. For the first time in my life, I put my needs above their's. With Rs 5000 in savings, I left for Kochi. I stayed in a hostel, and interviewed at a fitness center to work as a receptionist. I told the owner everything, and begged for a chance to prove myself, otherwise I'd have to go back. He hired me. My salary was Rs 11,000; it was my first victory in a long time.

I finally had the chance to discover 'me'—I got into fitness. I was just thirty-five kilos, and to put on weight, I began working out. My entire look changed—I even chopped off all my hair and donated it to cancer patients. I'd never cut my hair before, because men supposedly 'preferred' girls with long hair, but I no longer cared.

I was dating someone at the time, but I was unable to move ahead with him physically; I thought it was probably because of the past trauma. But when I connected with a girl from Belgium on Instagram, everything changed. I developed feelings for her ... feelings I couldn't explain. That was the first time I admitted to myself that I found women attractive and broke up with my boyfriend.

It didn't work out with the girl, but I wanted to explore my sexual orientation further and joined a dating app. I went on several dates—I still remember, when I had sex with a woman for the first time, I couldn't help but think, 'Oh my god, I'm so gay!' At first, I thought I was bisexual, but that wasn't the case—I identified as a lesbian. I found a piece of the puzzle I didn't even know was missing.

Over time, I decided to pursue fitness seriously and went to Bangalore for a course to become a trainer. I scraped up all my savings to pay for it. Once I got there, I only had a month's worth of money to survive on—I applied for jobs everywhere, but because my English wasn't that great back then, it was tough. Finally, I got a job at McDonald's. I began working there and studied to be a trainer on the weekends.

I was hand to mouth, when I got dengue, I had no money to get treated. So my previous gym owner's mom sent me money without me even asking; it was my first tryst with kindness. Slowly, I got better, got back on my feet and completed the course. I then got a job offer to work the front desk at a gym for Rs 18,000, with an offer to train under the owner who was ex-Mr. India. It was a once in a lifetime opportunity.

I didn't even have to give it a second thought—there was nothing left for me back in Kerala. So, I took up the job and began training. Over time, I got buff. I wanted to enter a bodybuilding competition, but needed a sponsor—someone who'd be willing to take a chance on me and shell out five to six lakhs.

With that thought, I posted a transformation photo on social media. A guy randomly stumbled on it and featured me on his blog—overnight I went from 3000 to 35,000 followers! It was just a snowball effect from then on. Someone else

I FILED A COMPLAINT AGAINST THEM IN THE WOMEN'S CELL FOR BURNING MY DOCUMENTS, AND NOT LETTING ME LEAVE.

on TikTok even made a transformation video on me, which went viral as well!

I got so much love and encouragement; I even got modelling and endorsement offers. But even though I needed the money, I turned them down—I don't want to be a model, I want to be recognized in the fitness industry. On the flip side, I also got hate from the Muslim community—they said things like, 'Allah is watching, you're going to burn in hell.' Honestly, if I'm going to go to hell for doing something I love, half the world will be chilling there with me!

I still haven't found a sponsor, but I'm not waiting around. I'm going to make it happen and sponsor myself. During the lockdown, I began an online diet program—I promoted it on social media; I got seventeen clients on the first day and today I got over 600 clients! I'm saving every penny.

I've realized that if you want something in life, you have to make it happen yourself; whether that's finances, family or love. I'm finally in a healthy relationship—I met Richa before the lockdown and we decided to quarantine

together. We're officially in a live-in relationship; we fight, we love but above all, we're happy—we recently adopted a dog!

I've left my life in Mukkam behind me. I still have no contact with my parents; I can't bring myself to forgive them for their decisions, especially my mother. I don't know what will happen decades down the road, but right now, I don't want them in my life.

In the last six years, it seems like I've lived a lifetime. Take it from me, there is no knight in shining armor; there is no one coming to save us. We have to do it ourselves—no one can save you, but you.

I'VE BEEN A TAXI DRIVER FOR OVER A DECADE, and work the night shift from 6 p.m. to 5 a.m. I'm a family man, and have a wonderful wife and two great kids back home. Through the years, I've met all kinds of passengers. Some who are really polite and considerate—they ask me how I'm doing or why I'm driving so late. On the other hand, I've also had passengers who've shown no regard for me at all. They'll get angry because they think I'm not driving fast enough, or because of any small thing that they think gives them the right to put me down. And I wish they'd understand that just because I'm only driving them somewhere, and they probably won't even remember my face again doesn't mean I'm not human. Every night I sit in the cab, praying for the safety of my family through the night, and most importantly hoping that I reach home safe, so that after a whole night of worrying, they can be at peace. I wish people just remembered that everyone, everywhere is going through something and if we showed just a little bit of kindness to anyone we come across, we would all get through it together.

I'VE BEEN TO BAMBAI ONCE IN MY LIFE–we went to Chowpatty and ate bhutta by the water. You know, people often talk about how Bambai is the city of dreams ... but it was too fast for me. Everyone's so busy; no one even gives you a second look. The whole time I felt so out of place. I wanted to come back here to my small hut and the greenery of the Khet. That city life isn't for everyone, I'll never go back.

TRIGGER WARNING It began when I was five years old. I was living in a joint family and every night my uncle, who's ten years older than me, would sexually abuse me. He'd grab me, touch my private parts and make me touch his. I was very scared and didn't understand what was happening, but he'd threaten to beat me if I told anyone. Slowly, it moved towards kissing and undressing and when I was nine, he asked me to give him a blowjob—I didn't even know what it was! He'd manipulate me and say things like, 'You have sexy eyes and such a pretty smile. If only you were a girl!' So I started imagining myself as a girl—I'd put on make-up, paint my nails and try wearing women's clothes, but didn't like any of it.

By the time I was fifteen, I realized I liked guys. I even started enjoying the time with my uncle; I was ashamed of how I felt—so I never told anyone. He'd twisted everything within me, but I knew it was wrong. After he got married, he'd still come to me from time to time. One night, I was studying for an exam when he came to me but I angrily shouted that it wouldn't happen anymore. And after that, he stopped. When I was seventeen, I started dating. I was seeing this guy who called me over to his place one evening.

When I reached, he wasn't alone—he had friends over. The entire evening, they made fun of me, called me names and tugged at my clothes. I was so humiliated—I went home and cried for hours! My homosexuality felt like a curse and I began to change my ways by walking straighter and being less expressive. I felt like I was all alone until I started researching the LGBTQ+ community. I found out that there were so many like me and even more, they were conquering life! Reading their stories inspired me to come out to my friends. When I told them, they didn't treat me any differently. For them, I was the intelligent, good-at-numbers Sudhakar!

OVER THE YEARS, I'VE GONE FROM HATING TO LOVING MYSELF.

They'd often tell me, 'You are more than just your gender, you know that, right?' Their understanding helped me accept myself! Today, I'm a taxation professor in a college and also the head of the Gender Sensitization Cell there. You wouldn't believe the questions my students ask me; but the truth is, the subject is still kept under wraps. Which is why I'm trying to raise as much awareness as I can.

Over the years, I've gone from hating to loving myself. Because he was the monster, not me—I was a child and he forced himself on me. I don't blame myself and I don't feel shame. Growing up, my mom always told me, 'As long as you're happy, you don't need to give a damn about the world.' So that's what I'm doing here—I'm telling my story, I'm letting the darkness go, I'm being me.

“

WE'RE ALL HERE AS EQUAL HUMANS—TO GO AND GROW THROUGH LIFE TOGETHER.

I'M AN EX HEADMASTER FROM KOLKATA. Moving to Pondicherry, with my wife, meant leaving behind the old-world charm and of course, the rasgullas! But I'm so glad I chanced upon this life. I used to teach Math but I always felt like the rigid education system wasn't working. So, after retiring, I came to Aurobindo Ashram, where I'm spending a life filled with books and of course, plenty of tiny tots as friends. I sit here, outside the school everyday and greet all these lovely kids! The kind of education I believe in is not just about learning lessons by rote, but understanding all nuances of 'what' and 'why' of things. Knowledge and growth is lifelong.

My kids are back home in Kolkata doing their thing, while I'm here, reading novels of all genres and living in a place that isn't divided by caste and grades. We're all here as equal humans—to go, and grow, through life together.

Kawasaki
Ninja

I COME FROM A MUSLIM FAMILY of scholars and Maulana's, but my first love has always been bikes and my father has been the most supportive. I rode my first bike when I was in the 9th grade and loved the feeling, but I got criticized for it only because I was a girl. So, I let it go for a while. I was twenty-two, when the rut of everyday life bore down on me—I was at my lowest. I remember leaving the house to give my CAT exam, when it hit me that I really didn't want to—so I came back.

Honestly, at the time, all I knew was that I wanted to do something I loved.

I took admission in Jamia Millia Islamia University because it gave me the opportunity to ride a bike to and fro. My parents were hesitant, but I convinced them. I had some money saved up—I pooled it in and with my father's help, bought my very first bike. Believe me, a Muslim girl, with her head covered, riding a bike, was an anomaly in college, but it was for the best, because some of the girls in my college started biking too! Around then, I tried joining a group traveling to Ladakh, but I overheard them saying I wouldn't be able to do it. I knew my capabilities and left it up for time to tell. That's when a newspaper wrote an article about me and slowly, I gained popularity—I even gave two TEDx talks. Soon after, I was approached by Indian Motorcycle, to ride with them for girl child education—from Kashmir to Kanyakumari! I rode the entire way on a 400 kg bike in record time! People started recognizing me on the street, and cops wanted to take selfies with me! When I began posting on social media, girls began sending me videos of them riding bikes! But I got trolled too. There have been times when guys on bikes try to prove they're better by trying to overtake me and in my head, I'm like, 'Aaja beta'. Before they know it, I've gone full throttle and zoomed away. That's not all—some people have even said that I won't get married because of biking! But honestly, when people ask me why, I just have one response—my religion, gender and clothes have nothing to do with my passion. I have five bikes but I also pray five times a day. I cover my head, but I wear a leather jacket and biker boots too. I'm doing what my heart tells me to—it's as simple as that. Why do I need a label or a tag to define me?

I HAVE FIVE BIKES BUT I ALSO PRAY FIVE TIMES A DAY. I PRACTISE MY RELIGION, I COVER MY HEAD, BUT I WEAR A LEATHER JACKET AND BIKER BOOTS TOO.

THAT'S WHAT I ALWAYS WANTED—TO BE SURROUNDED BY PEOPLE WHO GIVE ME FOOD FOR THE SOUL.

I **COME FROM A SMALL TOWN IN UTTAR PRADESH**, where language isn't given any importance. Every sentence is laden with cusses and there's no sense of culture; that's the society I grew up in. So, I had no role models to look up to and no recognition of what language or literature is. But, I was somehow drawn to stories; I just had no idea what to do about it.

But in 2017, I decided to randomly volunteer for an event called Jashn-E-Rekhta. Something told me that I should give it a shot.

Luckily, I got shortlisted and that's where my journey of falling in love with Urdu began.

Because I was new, I didn't stitch large dreams for myself. And that, probably, was the best part—when you don't have any expectations, you get the best experiences out of life. That's how I met Gulzar sahib—out of everyone, I was the one given the responsibility of escorting him to the event!

I can never forget those few hours I spent with him. He asked me if I would escort him to the restroom; he kept his hand on my shoulder throughout and it just felt like nothing I had experienced before—a man of such stature and knowledge, was with me.

I wanted to tell him how much I admired him, how he was such a beautiful director, how I had read and watched all his work—yet, I couldn't say a word. At last he asked me, 'Kya karte ho?' I meekly replied, 'Theatre'. Believe me, I hadn't been performing for quite some time, but the minute those words came out of my mouth, I decided I would pursue it! Later in the day, when he was having food, he asked me to also eat something. I put some food on my plate but could barely eat; such was the aura in the room! That day still feels so surreal.

Through Jashn-E-Rekhta, I also met people who were more well-read than me but willing to share that knowledge. That's what I always wanted—to be surrounded by people who give me food for the soul. And today, as a group, we mobilize Urdu literature through various art forms. We've been doing it for two years now and it's given me the life that I couldn't have even dreamt of five years ago—it's given me the gift of a precious language, of words.

FROM COOKING, CLEANING AND MAKING SURE THE CHILDREN'S FEES ARE ALWAYS ON TIME—EVERYTHING HAS BEEN IN PARTNERSHIP.

I **WAS TWELVE WHEN I WAS MARRIED**—my husband and I were both kids! Being married so young teaches you responsibility like nothing else—we both had to work to make ends meet. My first job was in construction—I used to get the mitti to build houses. I earned around Rs 13 a month back then! My husband and I were clear that we wouldn't have any children until we had a stable income ... so we came to Bombay and set up this vegetable stall forty years ago! Since the beginning, we've divided our work—I'm a good saleswoman, so when I'm here during peak hours, he handles the house—we even raised our children in shifts! From cooking, cleaning and making sure the children's fees are always on time; everything has been in partnership. Today, all our three children work in big companies ... they've made us so proud.

They earn a lot of money, but they know that we'll never stop working ... even though we don't need to. This is all I've known my entire life—it gives me purpose. I still feel the thrill when I earn good money in a day! What will I sit at home and do? This stall has given me freedom, to become something even though I've never studied. At first, I wondered if my children would feel ashamed to introduce us as vegetable vendors at their big work events ... but their pride is even more than ours. Recently, my daughter introduced me to her colleagues and said, 'my mother sells vegetables and everything I am today is because of her'—I was so happy, I couldn't even react!

AT EIGHTY-TWO, I'M STILL LEARNING. I FEEL LIKE THE 'RIGHT ADVICE' CHANGES OVER A PERIOD OF TIME—BUT THE ONE THING THAT REMAINS UNCHANGED IS THE DESIRE TO DO THE RIGHT THING.

I HAD A HAPPY CHILDHOOD, but as my brother and I got older, we faced a fair bit of ragging and personal discomfort because of our parent's divorce, which in those days wasn't as common as it is today. My grandmother brought us up in every way. Soon after when my mother remarried, the boys at school started saying all kinds of things about us—constantly and aggressively. But our grandmother taught us to retain dignity at all costs, a value that's stayed with me until today. It involved walking away from these situations, which otherwise we would have fought back against.

I still remember, after WW2, she took my brother and I for summer holidays to London. It was there that the values were really hammered in. She'd tell us, 'don't say this' or 'keep quiet about that' and that's where, 'dignity above everything else' really embedded in our minds. And she's always been there for us. It's difficult now to say who's right or wrong. I wanted to learn to play the violin, my father insisted on the piano. I wanted to go to college in the US, he insisted on the UK. I wanted to be an architect, he insisted on me becoming an engineer. If it weren't for my grandmother, I wouldn't have ended up at Cornell University in the US. It was because of her that even though I enrolled for mechanical engineering, I switched majors and graduated with a degree in architecture. My father was quite upset and there was a fair bit of rancour, but I was finally my own, independent person in college, and it was my grandmother who taught me that courage to speak up can also be soft and dignified.

After college, I landed a job at an architecture firm in LA, where I worked for two years. It was a great time—the weather was beautiful, I had my own car and I loved my job. It was in LA that I fell in love and almost got married. But at the same time, I had decided to move back at least temporarily since I had been away from my grandmother, who wasn't keeping too well for almost seven years. So, I came back to visit her and thought that the person I wanted to marry would come to India with me, but because of the 1962 Indo-China war, her parents weren't okay with her making the move anymore, and the relationship fell apart.

After I came back to Bombay, I was offered a job in Jamshedpur, at what is now Tata Motors. It was more of an internship—it seemed pointless. I was assigned for two weeks in this department, and two weeks in that department. But nobody was there to tell me what I was supposed to do. I spent six months trying to make myself seem useful. After that, I moved to Tata Steel. I got specific assignments, interesting jobs—I worked on the shop floor and in engineering. I was in Jamshedpur for six years, and by then architecture had simply become a hobby. But I was happy with the relaxed way of practicing architecture—like designing a home for myself.

In 1991, JRD Tata held the position of the Group Chairman, and the Chairman of the Tata Industries. The first company he stepped down from was Tata Industries.

HE WAS MY GREATEST MENTOR AND THE YEARS THAT HE WAS ALIVE.

People read that as, 'Ah, this is the first step of what JRD is going to do.' At first, there was no criticism, but when he decided to step down from Tata Sons, there was some vicious criticism. There were other aspirants for that position and so there was quite a vocal set of issues, of him having made the wrong decision of choosing me as his successor. I didn't fight back on the criticism, JRD had to do that, which he did not. The response from my side was that of silence. It was a very difficult period ... If you were to find the publications of that time, the criticism was personal—JRD got clubbed with nepotism and I was branded as the wrong choice. I was under a magnifying glass for a period of time. But through all of the criticism, through all that time that I spent on the shop floor were milestones that became my strongest pluses. All in all, it was a big move for me. I remember after the meeting in which I was appointed as the Chairman, I walked with JRD Tata to his office where he told his secretary that he had to move out of there now. I immediately said, 'No, J, you don't move out, this is your office as long as you want it.' He said, 'Where would you sit?' I said, 'Where I'm sitting today—I have an office down the hall and that's fine.' I was very lucky to have him there. He was my greatest mentor and the years that he was alive, I used to go into his office and say, 'J, I wish this had happened ten years ago, we have got such a great relationship.' He said he wished the same too! He was like a father and a brother to me, and not enough has been said about that.

Ever since, my life has been for and about growing the company. When I was appointed Chairman, it was widely believed that it was my surname that got me the position, but my focus was on creating something that was bigger than us all and on giving back, which has been entwined in the TATA DNA since the very beginning.

With Jamshedpur for instance, we realised that while our workers were thriving, the surrounding villages were still suffering. It became our goal to uplift their quality of life as well ... things like these came naturally to us. Even with the Nano—I remember seeing a family of 4 on a motorbike in the heavy Bombay rain. I knew I wanted to do more for these families who were risking their lives for lack of an alternative. By the time we launched the Nano, our costs were higher, but I had made a promise, and we delivered on that promise. Looking back, I'm still proud of the car and the decision to go ahead with it. That's what my life has been about—work became a lifestyle. I was either always at Bombay House or travelling, I guess that's why even though on the personal front I came close to marriage with 2-3 different partners, but I couldn't go through with it because they would have to change and adjust to my lifestyle and that didn't sit right with me.

Now that I'm retired, that lifestyle has changed again. People often ask if I'm truly 'retired', and to that I say—there's no doubt about it. I'm enjoying the separation from the company. I don't look at newspapers and worry about the bad stuff anymore. But let me tell you, retirement isn't about playing golf, or lying on a beach, reading whilst sipping on a cocktail. In fact, never before has the urge to do more, been greater. From affordable cancer treatment, to looking into making the lives in rural India easier—I'm looking forward to this chapter of making it happen at the Tata Trusts. I'm trying to enjoy myself to be honest. I'm spending time with friends—old and new, across all age groups, from whom I'm constantly learning.

At eighty-two, I'm still learning, so when you ask me to give a piece of advice, I feel like the 'right advice' changes over a period of time, but the one thing that remains unchanged is the desire to do the right thing. I'll say this—leave the advice aside and do what is the right thing, even if it isn't the easiest thing to do. When you look back at your life, that's what's going to matter the most. Doing the right thing.

“DO YOU SEE THIS TREE? IT PROVIDES OXYGEN WITHOUT ANY CONDITIONS OR EXPECTATIONS. IT JUST GIVES. WHEN PEOPLE BEND AND TOUCH MY FEET, I GIVE THEM BLESSINGS FROM THE DEEPEST PART OF MY HEART; I GIVE, AND DON'T NEED ANYTHING FROM THEM IN RETURN.

'UNCLE, WHERE DID YOU GET THIS WIG FROM?'

Do you know Aamir Khan? He was the Raja Hindustaani in all our lives! I got it from the set of the film. I worked there as a lightman. I have worked in many films! Do you remember Manoj Kumar's 'mere desh ki dharti ... '? I saw that happening in front of me!

Now, I'm working on a film called Tapan that stars Dilip Kumar in the lead. Watch out for it. I must be off now—lots to do!

EVER SINCE I WAS BORN, I've been missing the record of number one! I was the third heaviest baby to be born in Bombay hospital, second youngest kid to learn to drive at the age of six, and a few years later, I scored the second lowest score in the history of Marathi exams at Cathedral school. My childhood was spent at the Indian Express office with Dadaji. I grew up in that culture—home was office and office was home; in fact—the editor had moved into Dadaji's house at one point! After Dadaji passed, not much changed—I still loved that culture.

In fact, I would be at the office with dad straight after school and sometimes not come home until 1 a.m. I always knew that this is what I wanted to do, but when I was thirteen, our lives changed. Dad left us, and everything I had grown up taking for granted, changed. We'd only speak once a year on my birthday. And because he was the Chairman of the company, I became unsure about my career ... the one thing I'd been sure of my entire life.

But mom was my hero; she was still the vice chairperson of the company—so I would go to work with her after school and listen in on her meetings to learn. She brought me up loving a simple life. I didn't even realise that there's no money at home until I noticed that a painting was missing from our hallway—she sold it off just before I left for college.

In college, I studied business and marketing, but even my dad knew that I felt strongly about Dadaji's brand of journalism. Like most father- son relationships, I was keen on impressing dad and our time apart didn't change that—by the time I finished college we both knew that my future was with Indian Express. Through these years, I learnt the most from mom. She encouraged me to choose love over villainizing him or anyone else. Whatever his compulsions, I chose to let go. Whatever happened couldn't have been easy for him either. And looking back at our relationship's evolution, I am glad I did. Today, it's been seven years that dad and I have been working together. I have watched him turn the company around and the best part about working at the Express is the mutual respect we've developed for each other. We've had our highs and lows, but that's life—happiness is a choice, not anyone else's responsibility.

You can choose to remain stuck in the past or to pick love and move forward. I'm glad I chose the latter. Because that's why I'm where I'd hoped I would be—building and safeguarding Dadaji's legacy. And I've finally managed to snag the number one title—I recently became a father to the cutest baby in the world!

WHEN I WAS nine, my parents sat me down and told me I was adopted. They told me my mum died soon after I was born and nobody knew who my biological father was. They told me that I'd come out of my mother's heart and I would tease my elder sister and say, 'You came from mumma's belly but I came from her heart—so they love me more.'

But as I grew up, I wanted to know who my real parents were. My parents had no objections in letting me find my roots. I got to know from hospital documents that after my mother passed away, the hospital wrapped me in a cloth and left me outside the nearby police station until someone brought me to an orphanage. My mother used to volunteer in the same orphanage and adopted me when I was one-month old. She keeps telling me, 'There was an instant connection—the first time I saw you, I knew that I was destined to be your mother.'

But I still wanted to know more. I was frustrated about not knowing where I came from and used to vent in different ways. Sometimes, I would yell at my sister, at times my parents. I became obsessed with gathering old pictures, documents and trying to piece my life together. I had multiple theories woven inside my head but not knowing which one was true, was painful.

Finally, I decided to find out if the orphanage still existed. I took my help along, without telling my parents and went to the police station first. None of the old officers were working anymore and they refused to go through the files. I figured the orphanage had to be nearby and after a little searching, I found the right one.

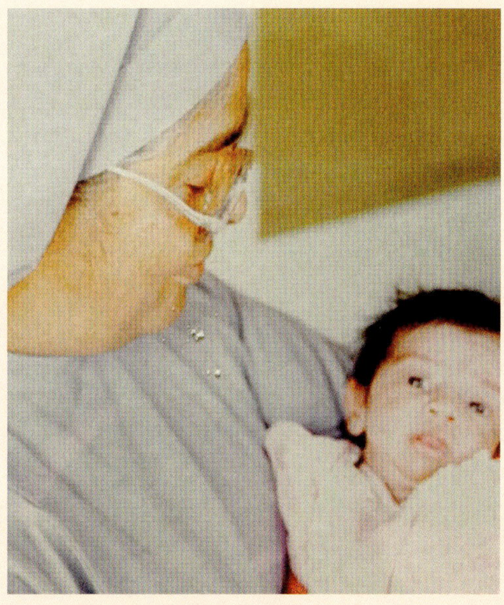

The minute I walked in, nostalgia hit me. It was like déjà vu—everything seemed so familiar. As I waited at the reception, an old lady walked in. I showed her some of my old pictures and she recognized me instantly. She was the one who had brought me there when I was a new-born baby. We hugged each other tightly and she enquired about my present life. That day, a lot of things changed in my life. As soon as I got back home, I confessed everything to my mother and started crying. My lifelong search for my biological parents ended—so did my self-pity. It's been five years since and I visit the orphanage often. Whenever I see a new child being admitted into the orphanage, I see a little version of myself in that baby. I guess it is all about family—this family that I chose, and the one God was kind enough to choose for me.

DEC 92 FEB 95
MAR 95 JUN 97
JUL 97
JUL 99
संजीव कनाल
SANJEEV KANAL

ALL OUR MEN CAMPED IN BUNKERS AND DURING THE NIGHT, THE SOUND OF GUNSHOTS AND BLASTS KEPT US AWAKE.

I WAS SIXTEEN WHEN I WATCHED THE PARADE at the National Defence Academy in Pune. That very moment, I turned to Dad and said, 'That's where I want to be.' When I wore the khaki wardi for the first time, it was a feeling like no other—I was ready to do anything for my country. During Rajiv Gandhi's Prime Ministership, I was posted as a helicopter pilot in Sri Lanka. My job was to move troops from one place to another. While evacuating casualties, there was a constant threat of enemy fire. I was newly married at the time and my wife would be worried sick. 'Promise me you'll come back?' she'd say. But she knew—it's nation first and everything else after that.

I was flying when I got the news about Rajiv Gandhi's assassination. But I didn't even have the time to react—I just carried on with my duty. When I was posted in Kashmir, I was prepared—I knew it was a major war zone.

There, every day we lived was a bonus day. Nobody knew when one of us would succumb to enemy shelling. All our men camped in bunkers and during the night, the sound of gunshots and blasts kept us awake. Every morning, we'd say a silent prayer aur fir hum sab 'Bharat Mata ki Jai' bolke nikal jaate the.

I stayed strong through it all, but it does take a toll on you. When the Kargil war broke out, I was just a few kilometres away from the battle zone. Once, enemy shelling hit our neighbouring bunker. I escaped, but lost many of my friends that day. Even today, when I think about it, I'm filled with remorse and inexplicable pain—I just can't get myself to talk about it.

After the war, I left Kashmir and over the years, I was posted across the length and breadth of the country. In 2017, I rose to the position of a Lieutenant General—the 2nd highest rank possible in the Indian Army. My final posting was in Chennai and I was responsible to train young men and women to be officers in the Indian Army. It made me so proud to train them to serve our country! It's been two weeks since I retired and came back to Pune. Now, I'm just busy renovating my room; I haven't gotten the time to reflect upon how I feel about staying at home all day. My wife keeps saying, 'You're going to be bored soon' but honestly, I'm happy to be reunited with my other family. In the last forty-two years of serving the nation, my family has often taken the backseat. Now, I want to make up for it. I have long chats with them, I help my wife in the kitchen and go for walks with my dog, Vodka. My mom and I play Uno in the evenings; she always wins. Of course, I miss the 6 a.m. alarms, camaraderie and the mess dinners but my patriotism lies in my heart, and I'll carry it with me till the end. For now, I'm going to make do by being the official chai maker at home!

I REMEMBER SITTING WITH A FOREIGNER, discussing his relationship. He was having a tough time in his marriage. I played his cards and gave him my advice. He was sceptical! But surprisingly, months later, he wrote to me about how he got a divorce and is now happily married to someone else. He even sent me a family photo and some cash to express his gratitude! Predicting people's future is my bread and butter. It runs in my blood—so I really do know what I'm doing! And with my parrot Meenakshi by my side, the goodwill is never ending. Whether or not you believe in destiny, fate, magic ... my parrot can never be wrong!

I USED TO WORK AT A BANK UNTIL I RETIRED. But after retirement, I found it difficult to pass my time—I'd been working my whole life. So, I decided to make and sell woollen items—socks, gloves, sweaters under a shack on the street—I loved it! I began meeting new people, negotiating and understanding the new world of business! But my son objected and questioned the prestige of this after my bank job. But I put my foot down and told him that I cannot be a kitchen fly whilst he toils as a daily wage labourer—I'm more than capable of still contributing to our family. And as for the 'status symbol' of this job I told him, 'koi kaam chota ya bada nahi hota' and that was the end of that conversation!

LIKE MOST FRESHERS IN COLLEGE, I wanted to be famous! I also felt like getting 'good grades' wasn't the way to go about it. So, I asked my parents if I could go for a forty-five day long 'educational' trip to Egypt. Of course, they said no. So I had my Plan B ready and decided to make YouTube videos. Two of my friends and I began shooting for our first video where I was playing a madman. We began roaming the streets of Kolkata and ended up scaring an aunty—she fainted! We splashed some water on her face, and when she woke up, she warned us not to try this on anyone else! But still we decided to pull one more prank, which totally backfired. A 6 ft tall guy grabbed our cinematographer. We had no other choice but to run away, while he was getting beaten by an angry crowd. The aunty who'd fainted was there too! Turns out, she was an international lawyer and threatened to get us arrested! We were there for eight hours, before my father tracked us down and got us out of there. He was obviously shaken by what had happened and asked me what I wanted ... that's how I got my Egypt trip!

TRIGGER WARNING I was seventeen when I realized that the constant sadness that I felt within me, wasn't something everyone felt. School was crappy—I didn't have friends. In 10th grade, a group of the popular kids accused me of spreading a rumour. Because of that, I isolated myself which turned into anger at home. I remember one time, my mother forgot to buy a chocolate and I was so mad that I started to yell and break things. My parents were worried, especially when I wouldn't eat for extended periods of time; I never told them how I actually felt—I blamed it on stress.

I started cutting myself by the end of my first term. I would wear long-sleeved shirts to hide my arms. I would doodle 'I am a loser' on my books. I would write poetry; it helped me emote.

Then, one day my parents saw my cuts and were furious. They wanted me to get help, but I flat out refused.

My big moment of realization happened when we went to Rajasthan for a wedding. I refused to leave the house and made a big scene—it made my mother cry. I remember thinking, 'what am I doing to my parents?' The next day, I asked them to find a therapist.

It's been a few months since that trip to Rajasthan and I know I have a long way to go in my healing journey ... but my scars are there to remind me, that even at my lowest, I didn't break, so there's nothing I can't overcome.

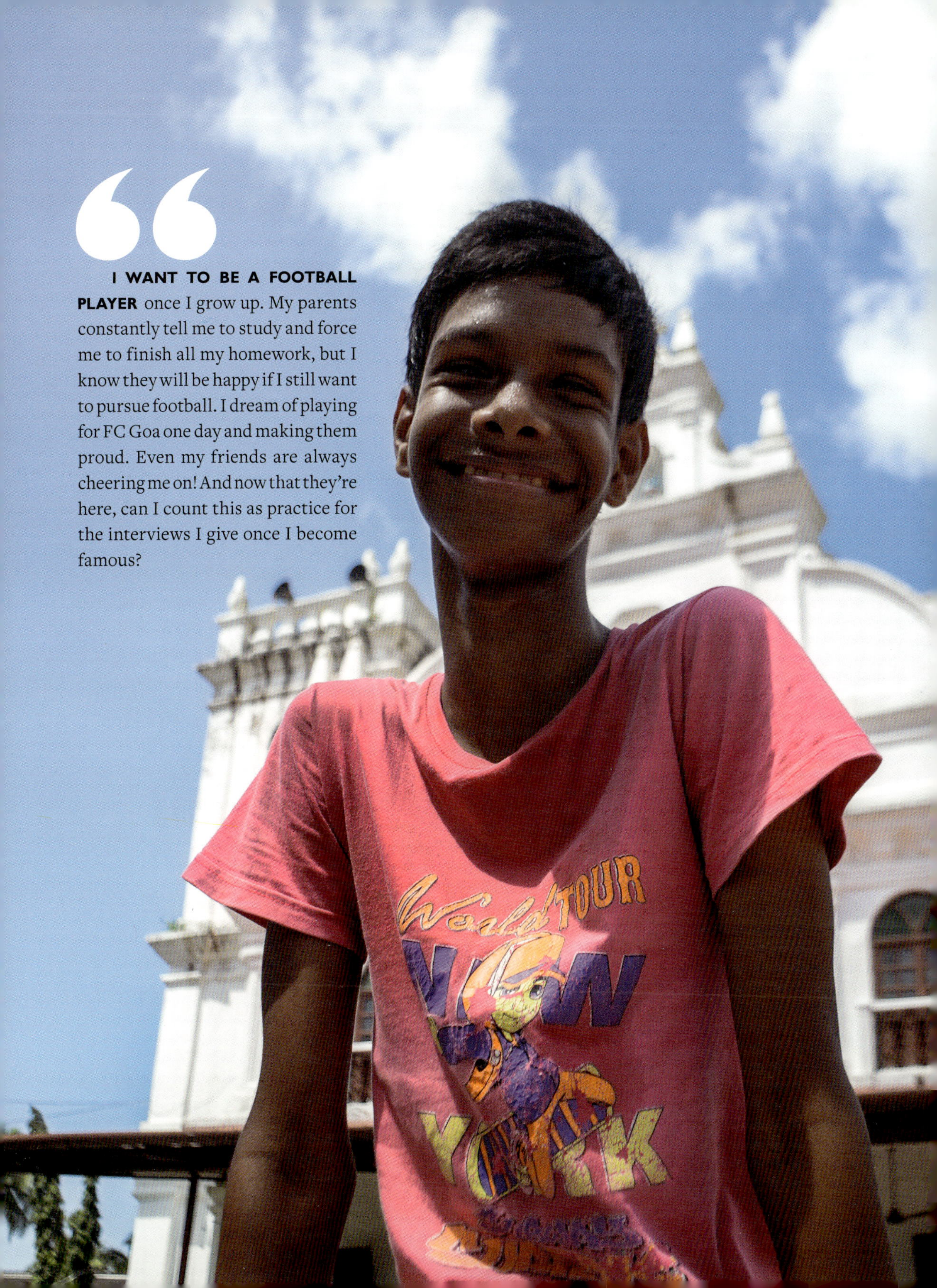

"

I WANT TO BE A FOOTBALL PLAYER once I grow up. My parents constantly tell me to study and force me to finish all my homework, but I know they will be happy if I still want to pursue football. I dream of playing for FC Goa one day and making them proud. Even my friends are always cheering me on! And now that they're here, can I count this as practice for the interviews I give once I become famous?

GROWING UP, MY PARENTS WERE alcoholics—still, they tried being good parents. But eventually as the drinking became routine, I was sent to live with my aunt at the age of five. I felt lonely because the other kids at school always had their parents around. I tried making friends, but I was constantly teased—kids would say, 'You have chicken legs' and 'You look so unhealthy'. I'd call my mom and cry to her and while talking to her helped, the comments still mentally drained me.

This went on for years, until 2015, when I decided to move to Bombay to start over. I applied for a BMM course and started blogging on the side. I loved fashion, but never gave it a shot because I let those comments get to me. I felt I wasn't 'pretty enough'. But when I started posting pictures, I got comments about how good my fashion sense was and how confident I looked—it felt so much more fulfilling than just being pretty!

Things were so much better—until two years back when my father passed away because of alcoholism. We'd just started getting close, so it was heartbreaking to watch him go. I couldn't understand why all this was happening to me, but the one thing that kept me going was blogging. I used it to distract myself from everything that was going on, and it worked.

I'm now a twenty-two year-old fashion blogger, who's working hard to ace college. From being labelled as 'too dark' and 'too skinny', today I'm working with brands like Adidas, Nike, Maybelline and many more. I make my own money and plans are on the way to start my own clothing line!

Also, I've met so many new people and have so many friends who don't judge! I love my life. Initially, I'd use blogging as an escape. But now, it's become the centre of my life, and honestly, it feels surreal to have something that I don't have to depend on anyone for, the one thing that's just 'mine'. And now, when I get hate comments, I just post a few extra pictures that day to shut the haters up, because I mean ... I can.

TODAY I'M WORKING WITH BRANDS LIKE ADIDAS, NIKE, MAYBELLINE AND MANY MORE. I MAKE MY OWN MONEY AND PLANS ARE ON THE WAY TO START MY OWN CLOTHING LINE!

I'M 100 YEARS OLD, but I remember the first time I saw her so vividly. A panditji matched our kundlis, so my family and I went to see her. I still annoy her that I only went ahead because of my parents. But between us, she was so beautiful, I couldn't stop staring. I didn't think she'd say 'yes' to a man ten years older than her, but the elders talked, baat pakki ho gayi and we were married.

There was no honeymoon phase; we were thrust into a joint family with strict rules. With little money to ourselves, every day was a struggle. My brother bought us clothes, because I didn't have enough to even buy her a saree. But she never complained. She supported me as I worked in the family business and looked after my health; I wasn't allowed to skip my walk at 5.30 a.m.!

I'd drive around South India delivering agarbattis for three weeks every month, but she never let me feel guilty; she'd pack my bags and tell me not to worry about her. I trusted her so much that I only felt right about a decision if she approved it. So, even though everyone thought it was a reckless move, she stood by me when I left the family business to start my own. She gave me courage and said, 'We'll get through it together'.

I dreamed of giving her our own home. I clocked long hours at the office, while she looked after our daughters and ran the house. We didn't have much, but she made me feel like the richest man in the world when she sat by my side after a long day. After seventeen years of saving every penny, we made that dream a reality.

We built a new life in this home. Every morning, I'd make the bed, while she made the softest dosas. In the evenings, she'd pick out flowers from our garden, and I'd peek through the newspaper to gaze at her. Carnatic music always filled the air at home and every sunday, we had a date at a concert!

After our daughters were married, we took our first trip abroad. I was scared of getting lost and insisted on sitting in the tour bus, but she said, 'nothing will happen, let's go' and took me all around town! I've lived a century now, and I still need her advice on the smallest of things. My kids often tease me and ask, 'Did your wife say 'yes' to this?' and we both laugh!

Last year, on our 71st anniversary, we renewed our vows because two kids, four grandkids and two great grandkids later, one lifetime is simply not enough to celebrate our love.

Note: Mrs. Rukmini Setty passed away as this book went into print.

EVERY GENERATION IN MY FAMILY has at some point sat here and sold fish. It's the only thing I've known since childhood. Currently, it's on me. It's how we've earned our livelihood and how we will continue to do so. But I've decided to break that streak and end it with me. My children can help me out here but I want them to study and become whoever they want to be. But I don't see myself doing anything other than this. Right now, my biggest problem is this cat that sits by me every day. It waits for me to turn away so it can nibble on my fish but I've got my eye on him—I may even enjoy this cat and mouse game! Other than that, I'm very happy!

I'VE HAD THIS SHOP FOR FORTY YEARS. All day long I'm surrounded by hundreds of Gods—almost every customer who comes to me believes in a different God. Even I have a dharma guru; I put my faith in his preaching but I've always believed that in the end there is only one almighty, it doesn't matter whether we find him through the Quran, Gita or Bible. Because he made so many different kinds of people, he gave them different forms of worship, that's the only truth I know.

WHEN I WAS BORN, the doctor told my parents that there was a chance I would never walk or talk, in addition to being visually impaired—little did he know that I was going to turn out to be a complete chatterbox! When I first applied to school, they rejected me because they thought that 'I would spoil the other normal children'! But that's where they were wrong—I was normal! I went to another regular school and blossomed. I still remember dressing up in a sari for a fancy dress competition—I wanted it to be perfect, so I practiced walking on stage—and I won first prize! My teachers also went out of their way to keep me involved—during Dahi Handi, one of my teachers held me up to the pot so I could feel the celebrations! Even during Diwali, my friends would sit beside me and describe the colours of the crackers in the sky! In the 7th standard, I won the Bal Shree President's Award. I wasn't at school when they announced it, but apparently, my classmates jumped up and down on the benches! I received my award from Dr. Abdul Kalam at the Rashtrapati Bhavan! College was a whole other world. My mother would travel with me by train all the way to Marine Lines and then walk me to and from college—and when lectures were cancelled, she'd have to turn back and come back for me! But family has always come first, it's the biggest rule of our house. In fact, before my sister got married she told her fiancé that I was her number one! Even though my sister now lives in London, she's been my biggest support throughout my job application process. For the last two years, I've been working at a bank as a clerk. I've obviously had my challenges too, I've had instances where customers sometimes complain to management because they think I'm sleeping, but my colleagues stand up for me!

I've never allowed any of this to bring me down, honestly, it just makes me want to work harder. A few years ago I realized I had a story I wanted people to know, so I even wrote a book.

The doctor had sealed my fate on the day I was born, but today, I'm an author, I'm completely financially independent, I have a job that I love, and I'm surrounded by people who believe in me, and my dreams. I'm more than 'that blind girl' and I'm more than any label or tag. I'm more than my 'disability', and I'm more than my supposed 'limitations'. I *see* that every day and I wish the world could *see* it too.

A FEW YEARS AGO I REALIZED I HAD A STORY I WANTED PEOPLE TO KNOW, SO I EVEN WROTE A BOOK.

HE'D MOVED TO INDIA JUST A FEW WEEKS before we met! We were sitting at different tables in a cafe; I was brainstorming with my team. Little did I know, he was eavesdropping the entire time. He came over to my table after everyone left, and gave me a few suggestions on how to improve my business! He kept talking ... but I was already a goner.

I had a crush on him from that very first day. I would ask him random questions regarding work—just so I could talk to him a little bit longer. We became friends quickly. I introduced him to a whole new world ... my brave new world.

Soon after, I told him how much I liked him, and how much I loved spending time with him, he told me that he was straight. He considered me his best friend, but that was all he had to offer. Heartbroken or not, I wasn't about to pass that up. I really don't know whether we would've worked out as a couple. But he's stuck with me for life now—I mean, how can he dump his best friend?

I'VE BEEN GROWING MY MOUSTACHE for over thirty-five years—it's thirty-two feet long! I had once visited a temple in 1975 and met a man there whose moustache was seven feet long! People treated him like a celebrity; I wished to feel the same way too! So, I joined the Forest Department as a driver and decided to grow my moustache to stand out. It worked; tourists stare at me more than the scenery! My manager told me, 'You are our star attraction!' That motivated me to grow it further!

But many women rejected me for not wanting to shave. When I met my wife, she said, 'Why would I want to change who you are?' I immediately said, 'I'd love to marry you!'

It took her time to adjust to walking around with me as people would take our pictures. But despite that, never once has she requested me to shave. It's cumbersome to maintain it too; in the mornings, my family would take three hours to clean it with oil! I'd often get late to work because of it. When my boss would ask, 'Why are you late?' I'd reply, 'Sir, I had a bad moustache day!'

Despite some inconveniences, I walk about with pride. My village calls me 'Moustache Man'. ' And as the news about my moustache spread, I was offered jobs to show it off at events;! Children in my locality often use it as a skipping rope. Now, I'm trying to grow it even longer! And when people ask me why I don't shave, I say, 'The beauty of men from Rajasthan comes from their moustache!'

I COME FROM A HUMBLE FAMILY. My father sold newspapers and my mother is a homemaker. I was enrolled in a private school, but as a slum dweller. It was a challenge but also a big opportunity for me to fulfil my parents' dreams. The most comforting thing about living there was the fact that no street lamp or high-rise building stopped me from viewing the bright stars in the night sky.

When I was 10-years-old, the curiosity to know what goes on in outer space took over me. After a year of questioning my teachers and getting vague replies, I enrolled in an astronomy workshop at school. That day, I witnessed the beauty of Saturn's rings through a telescope and I just knew that that's what I wanted to do for the rest of my life.

I even told my parents that I wanted to become an astronomer, but they didn't think it was a sustainable career option. Even then, my curiosity couldn't be contained.

I started saving my pocket money by skipping meals and walking to school to buy myself a telescope worth Rs 5000! When my parents found out they didn't talk to me for days—they thought it was a big waste of money!

But I was thrilled and kept learning through my telescope. When I was fourteen, I discovered an asteroid! The news was published in newspapers and my father was speechless. I was the only person from our slum who had been featured in the papers!

Eventually, I started getting invited to universities as a lecturer and in my first month I made Rs 30,000! I also began giving Ted Talks and amassed so much knowledge on astronomy that I didn't even realise that I had a career as an Astronomy lecturer! That's how I make money and study side by side.

AND ALL OF THIS WAS POSSIBLE ONLY BECAUSE I REMAINED CURIOUS AND FOLLOWED MY PASSION.

Recently, my parents and I were travelling back from Varanasi and had booked train tickets, but I bought all of us flight tickets with my own money! It was the first time my parents sat on an airplane and my mother got the window seat. She was so happy and proud.

After the flight, I took them to a restaurant and paid for the food from my own pocket—that was the proudest I've ever seen my dad.

And all of this was possible only because I remained curious and followed my passion. That's why today I've given talks internationally and am financially independent at nineteen! My big dream is to have my own observatory and make ground breaking discoveries!

But before that, I have something special coming up in January—I'm taking my parents to stay in a hotel where my dad once worked as a security guard! All these small moments for us makes me feel that, as a family, we've already touched the stars.

TRIGGER WARNING I got married when I was seventeen years old, to someone who was twenty-four. My husband and I didn't get along from day one—so I knew I had to take care of myself. I started a small business of selling garments from home and made enough for the house, but that irked my husband. He was a rickshaw driver, he wouldn't earn. He'd just extort money from people, bring random men home and drink late into the night. He'd even threaten to kill me if I ever came in his way. Once when we got into an argument, he took a knife and slashed my face. I was in a horrible state. But my mother refused to let me come home, because my sisters wouldn't be able to marry if I did.

Just a few months later, I gave birth to my first baby girl. Once, when the baby was crying a lot, he got so annoyed that he dumped her into a garbage bag and was going to throw her away. I threatened to call the police, and that's when he stopped.

After my second daughter was born, his behaviour became worse. He'd beat me and my daughters both. One night, he told me, 'You have so much attitude because you earn money, one day I'll make sure you're in a state where you're ashamed to step out'. I went to my mother's house, asking her to save me. But she told me not to react and go back home.

I ALWAYS WANTED TO MAKE IT BIG IN LIFE, AND I'M STILL GOING TO DO THAT.

So with nowhere to go—I went back to him. That night, while I was sleeping, he threw acid on my face. I woke up feeling like I was on fire. My skin was melting and I was half dead. The neighbours heard my painful screams, so they came and rushed me to the hospital. But the damage was done. I spent four months in the hospital, but nobody from my family came to help me. Thankfully that's when Acid Survivors Saahas Foundation found me and funded my treatment.

I filed a police complaint and my husband was thrown in jail, but each day I'd spend wanting to kill myself. My own daughters didn't want to come to me, people who I knew in the locality refused to talk to me or even give me a place to stay—only because of how terrible I looked. When I was discharged from the hospital, the NGO helped me send my kids to a boarding school, because I couldn't afford to keep them.

My husband and my family did what they wanted to do—ruin my life and have nothing to do with me. But one thing they haven't been able to do is break my morale. I can't step out without wearing a scarf, I'm not getting a job or a place to stay, I'm fighting this battle all alone. But this is not the end for me. I always wanted to make it big in life, and I'm still going to do that—only now, I'll always have my scars reminding me to never give up.

I COULD NEVER STAY PUT IN ONE PLACE—I love travelling! After I finished my studies, I cycled like a maniac from one place to another; I randomly took my cycle and set out on a trip from England to Morocco. I picked up some culinary skills along the way. All the while, my parents had no idea about my shenanigans. In fact, my father wanted me to take over his farm and work on a tractor, but it was my mother who inspired me to cook. She's a free spirit, like me, and I wanted to do what she did, so I decided to do everything for her! I worked in France as a chef, stumbling my way around dishes I had no idea how to cook, then as a chef on a yacht for a Russian billionaire. Then I somehow ended up in the Andamans, and then Mumbai for my next big adventure.There, I ended up chatting with a woman in a coffee shop, which led me to Pondicherry. I've been here for more than six months—this is the longest I've stayed anywhere. But for the first time, I don't want to leave; this café is my baby now. And I have to admit, one of the biggest reasons I'm here is because of my team. They all come from different places and backgrounds, speak different languages, but in the kitchen we're all one. I think I've found a family—and because of them, for once, my feet are firmly planted on the ground. And I guess that's why they say it's family that grounds you—who knew I'd find mine thousands of miles from home, in the cozy town of Pondicherry?

WE'RE WAITING FOR AN auto to take us to the train station so that we can go back home to Rajasthan. A few days back, I ran away from my husband's house. It all began when I came home after a long day of working in the fields and was a little late to serve supper. My mother in law was so angry—she demanded that I quit work and stay at home the whole day to serve her and the family. I told her that I didn't want to quit and that my work gave me purpose. I tried telling her that I'd do better to balance things, but before I knew it my husband slapped me thrice and told me to never speak to his mother like that again.

So, I ran away and my sister here came with me to make sure I wasn't alone. Right now, we're just waiting for our sandwich before we leave for Rajasthan, where our mother lives. Honestly, I don't know what the plan is when I get there, but I do know that I don't need to be married just so that I have someone to feed me—I'm capable of feeding myself and my mother and sister. So that's what I'll focus on—my purpose, and standing up to those who tell me that I'm only 'good enough' to sit at home and do nothing with my life!

WHEN I WAS PREGNANT with Rudra, everything was perfect. All of the check-ups and tests, were normal.

When I finally gave birth to Rudra, we were so happy. But when he was born, he wasn't breathing—they immediately shifted him to the NICU.

We didn't know what was happening. That's when a doctor said, 'Your son's got water retention in his brain, he's going to be a vegetable his whole life, if he survives'. We were devastated. For nine days, Rudra couldn't breathe on his own. And every day the doctor would inch us towards ending his life. 'There's no point', is what we'd hear all day. Although our entire family stood by us, we didn't know what to do.

But on the ninth day, Rudra started breathing on his own! For me it was a sign, he was meant to be by our side. We got him home and started equipping ourselves with all the information that we needed to take care of him.

Even something as simple as breastfeeding was a problem, because he couldn't hold himself up. But we regularly took him to therapy. He was a diaper baby till he was about eight years-old, and he couldn't even sit up straight. Once I'd put him on the bed, and was looking in the other direction. After five minutes when I turned towards him again, he sat up by himself! Small things like this were the biggest milestones for us.

But things were not always rosy. He never had any friends. I remember when I used to take him to parks, I actually had parents come up to me and say, 'Please don't get him out, it's not good for our kids to see him.' It used to break my heart, but I couldn't let it get to me. Now that Rudra is older, there are still things he can't do but we're trying everything we can to give him the best life possible. Recently we took him on his first ever trip to Kerala. We thought he'll get overwhelmed and we may have to come back. But it was the opposite! He didn't complain or cry at all, he was enjoying all the sights!

My husband and I work, and Rudra goes to a special school. In the evening when we come back, we watch his favorite movies—and that's the best part of our day. Because when I see all of us being so happy together, I feel grateful. More than us, he put up a strong fight, he powered through and is still doing so every single day. He deserves a shot at life just as much as we do and I'm glad that we didn't give up on him—he's my warrior.

MORE THAN US, HE PUT UP A STRONG FIGHT, HE POWERED THROUGH AND IS STILL DOING SO EVERY SINGLE DAY.

I REMEMBER I WAS NINETEEN, and in the first year of my college. I was excited to start a career, but my family decided to get me married. In my community, girls were not encouraged to be independent.

My husband was the youngest in his family, so I had a lot of elders to take care of. I'd barely find time for myself. Within a few years, both my kids were born. I'd be devoted to them and the household chores from morning to evening—and by the time it all ended, I'd be exhausted. Amidst this, I found myself a hobby. I started designing Ridas—cotton Hijabs, for my daughter.

I'D BEEN A HOUSEWIFE FOR SO LONG THAT THEY DIDN'T THINK I'D BE OKAY, OUT THERE IN THE WORLD.

One day at the mosque, my daughter was wearing one of my Ridas, when a lady complimented the design, and asked me to make one for her daughter!

After that, through word of mouth, people in my community started approaching me. Soon the orders increased so much that I made enough money to be financially stable. I even contributed to my children's pocket money. Through it all, my husband was my pillar of strength. He'd come with me to buy fabric and manage my finances. But my relatives weren't as supportive. I remember one of them asked me to make a dress for her daughter's wedding. I put so much of my hard work into it, but they just pointed out faults that weren't there and told me I didn't do a good job. I didn't let that deter me, though.

I'd finally found my place and I wasn't going to let it go. Soon after, I got to know that the shop I used to source fabrics from was going to shut down. I saw an opportunity there. I went home and asked my husband if we could buy the shop. My husband agreed, but not my children. They didn't think I'd be okay, out there in the world, all alone. People even questioned my husband on why he was wasting so much time and money. But he never hesitated. We took the plunge and bought the shop—it's been two and a half years since. I stand in the shop alone, deal with customers and traders every day. Looking at how hard I work, all my kids support me thoroughly now.

I started my business when I was fifty and I'm doing everything in my power to be more successful than ever. My most gratifying moment was when I was able to contribute to my daughter's overseas education.

It's moments like these that drive me to push the roadblocks away. I'm lucky to have a husband and a family that lifts me up and makes me feel like I'm capable of anything. I'll do everything it takes to make myself, and them proud.

I LIKE TO DO CHAP CHAP IN THE RAIN.
DO YOU LIKE GETTING WET IN THE RAIN?
YES, BUT MUMMA FORCES ME TO WEAR A RAINCOAT . . . SO WHEN SHE'S NOT LOOKING, I TAKE IT OFF AND RUN TO DO CHAP CHAP!

'WHAT'S THE HAPPIEST MOMENT OF YOUR LIFE?' I WANT TO SAY IT WAS WHEN I PROPOSED TO MY HUSBAND. BUT ACTUALLY, I WAS THE HAPPIEST WHEN I GOT A SMALL ROLE IN A FILM ... DON'T TELL HIM THAT BUT!

I'VE BEEN WORKING most of my life. In the beginning, I needed money to run my household, then I needed money for my kids and now that I'm a grandmother, I'm saving up for my grandkids. I have five children and thirteen grandchildren, earlier there were fifteen in all, but a few years back two of them died of swine flu.

My son was already going through a financial crisis when tragedy struck. It was a very difficult time for him and my daughter-in-law. I couldn't bear to see them in that state, so I took care of all the medical expenses. People tell me that now I need to stop working, but I want to be able to provide for my babies, whenever they need me so I'll continue to work until my body is willing. After all, a mother will always be a mother, no matter how old her children get.

MY MOTHER'S FAMILY LIVES in Faisalabad, Pakistan. She married my father when she was twenty; her parents had to flee to Pakistan right after. She hasn't been able to see them since because they never got a visa to enter India. And my father never had enough money for her to travel, so I've never met them.

But my mother always told me stories of how they would write letters to her every month. My grandparents always sent me and my siblings one small Dairy Milk chocolate with the letters. I remember waiting for the mailman to come home just so I could have my chocolate! Now that I have grandchildren, I make sure that every Sunday I give them one Dairy Milk—just to show them how much I love them and to make sure that they'll always remember their baba, even when I'm not around.

TRIGGER WARNING: Graphic content We found a baby girl six months ago in a plastic bag that was in a dog's mouth. A passer-by saw movement in the bag and called us—we rushed her to the hospital. She couldn't breathe and had been fed poison, and her treatment took seven months.

Every day, I'd visit her. It broke my heart to see her in the incubator, being fed through a pipe. Finally, a few days back, she was discharged and ever since, she sleeps next to me at night. I started Unique Home in 1993 to provide orphaned and abandoned girls a better life. That year, we found a baby girl in a dustbin. Ants were eating her skin and she was unconscious, so we took her to the hospital. She was there for a month, but recovered quickly. When I got her home, she was just a toddler, and for twenty-five years, I raised her—right from preschool to college. Today, she's doing her PHD abroad! But that was the day I decided to never let these abandoned girls feel like orphans again. Over the past twenty-seven years, I've rescued hundreds of girls, but more than that, I'm a mother to so many!

We share a typical mom-daughter relationship—I scold them if their room is messy or if they're eating junk. And they quickly make it up by making chai for me or an apology card!

Yet, there are days when I'll come across a case that shakes me to my core. Recently, we brought home five sisters whose mother was beaten to death by their father after their youngest sister was born. When I read about it in the paper, I couldn't sleep all night. I spoke with the authorities and got them home.

EVERYONE KEEPS TALKING ABOUT GENDER EQUALITY AND SHATTERING THE GLASS CEILING. ”

In the beginning, they wouldn't eat, talk or sleep and the eldest one kept saying, 'Take me home.' To calm her down, I'd tell her, 'Your mom told me that we are your family and I'm your mom now.'

Slowly, we integrated them into counselling sessions, painting classes and studies, and they started opening up to the other girls. Six months later, they're eating well and now the eldest one says, 'I never want to leave!'

Truth is, I'll never stop my kids from doing what they love. Like one of my thirteen year-olds is a great runner, andwe want to hire a trainer for her. If sports is her thing, I want to see her bring laurels home! I want them to understand that they can overcome any hurdle—and that this world is a much better place than the one they came from.

In this day and age, everyone keeps talking about gender equality and shattering the glass ceiling. But tell me one thing, how will girls ever reach there if they are never given the chance? If they're left to die simply because they're girls?

I GOT MARRIED AT TWELVE—It was considered normal back then! But I feel so lucky to have grown up with this generation. I absolutely love how outspoken youngsters today are! I think I was meant to be born in this generation, because I've not tolerated any injustice ever since my marriage. Once, this young man, a far-off relative I knew was in love with a Muslim woman. His mom was furious. When I heard about this, I told her, 'your son has looked after you all these years, and you obviously love him. So why wouldn't you want his happiness? ' I managed to convince both families!

This other time, I heard screaming noises from our neighbours' house. I found out that the middle-aged woman living there was being beaten by her nephew. I went there, and told him to watch himself. I got him arrested and told him, 'If I see you beating her again, I will break your hands'.

I fail to understand what joy people get from dampening others' lives.

Why should one have any power over who they love, what caste or class they should marry, or what they choose to do with their lives? Mein toh bas yehi kehti rehti hoon—jeeyo, aur jeene do yaar—tum apna dekho, hum apna dekhenge!

I'M COMING FROM DARGAH SHARIF and honestly, I don't know where I'm going next. But this has been me all my life. I'm what people refer to as a 'banjara!' I'm originally from Bikaner, but mera na koi ghar hai na thikana. I go to a city, stay there for a few months, do odd jobs like waiting at restaurants or labour work and then move on to the next place. Still, I've had days where I've slept on the road or under a tree, but I take that also in my stride. After all, I wanted to experience life in its entirety—with all its highs and lows! Once, I met this foreigner, who, like you, was somehow interested in speaking to me. I told her who I was and what I did.

Apparently, she was learning Hindi then, so after hearing my story, she looked at me and said, 'Musafir!' I guess that's who I am—a musafir! There are many who have given me other such titles—nomad, wanderer, gypsy. But I think I'll stick with Banjara—meri image ke saath jaata hai!

I'M MOST PROUD OF TRANSFORMING INTO THIS WOMAN WHO CAN AFFORD THE LIFE OF HER DREAMS!

WHEN I WAS SIX, my best friends were the shampoos in my bathroom—I'd have conversations with them. I didn't have friends in school and was alienated for having a humble background—my brother and I were only allowed two new clothes per year. I remember every night, I'd pray to wake up to a closet full of shoes.

I was also shamed for my crooked teeth and skinny body. Family, friends, teachers and strangers called me, 'Bag of bones, kaali lakdi and sukhi dandi'. People thought that it was funny to say that I would fly away with the wind—it wasn't. I started battling anxiety and I didn't even know that it was called anxiety.

The bullying worsened in the 11th grade. Some kids would crowd around me, taunt me and throw chalks at me. During a farewell party for seniors, I wore an outfit I'd bought from my savings—but I wasn't aware that there was a dress code. My teacher paraded me around in front of other teachers and said, 'Dolly you look hideous, get out of my sight'. I was even asked to get off stage in front of everyone because I looked 'ugly'. I wanted to break down, but every time I'd stop myself.

So, I moved to Delhi to start over. Around that time, I fell in love with a boy miles away—he came to meet me for the first time but ghosted me right after. I blamed myself and shut people out for a year.

Eventually, I realised that I didn't want to feel that way ever again, so I shifted my focus to being financially independent. I started selling clothes from Sarojini online and emceeing at malls. I avoided going out for dinners and movies to save more.

My old love for fashion came out as well—I created a fashion blog, worked as a stylist and started making videos. I created characters, just like I did with those shampoo bottles as a child.

Life has come full circle. I moved from my small hometown to renting my own place in Delhi and from being bullied for my clothes to international fashion trips. But I'm most proud of transforming into this woman who can afford the life of her dreams; all without changing a thing about herself!

To this day, I get hate but it doesn't affect me anymore—a while ago, I overheard two girls calling me 'ugly' on the metro, but as I moved away, another girl came up and asked me for a selfie. There will always be haters, but I choose to focus on the positive; on the itch that's allowed me to get to where I am today. And this is a pretty amazing place to be—after all, my crooked teeth and skinny body got me from two pairs of clothing to a walk-in closet ... mic drop.

MY FATHER'S AN AUTO RICKSHAW DRIVER and my mother used to work at other people's houses. My childhood was filled with a fascination for people, objects, skies, light. Soon I realised that I was a photography fanatic, but because photography wasn't considered a 'good career option', I was made to study BCom and straight out of college, I got a job. I was happy for my parents ... just not for me.

I'd work throughout the week and on weekends, I'd go out and seek—a corner, a person ... to get that one perfect picture. I'd post it all on Instagram. Things were finally looking up, when—I lost my job. I decided to not tell my parents. For three months, I pretended I had a job when in fact I was looking for photography assignments. Slowly, I became a known name and was waiting for the right moment to tell my parents. I was at the beach with a friend when massive amounts of plastic washed up on the shore! She suggested we take a picture of it—which later, I uploaded too. Hours later, when I got home, my mom showed me the same picture—it was forwarded to her on WhatsApp. I told her I'd clicked it and rushed to check my phone! It had gone viral! That day, the world convinced my parents for me. Today, international brands want me as their photographer! But what I'm proudest of is the fact that I contribute an even better amount at home and finally my parents can rest, have a better lifestyle, be happy and never worry about anything again!

I GREW UP WATCHING MY MOTHER WORK and take care of the household. I resolved to be independent too. I worked before getting married and continued after. But, it was getting difficult managing full-time work.

Then, I saw an announcement in the newspaper—both men and women could now have taxi permits. So, I passed the driver's test and bought a taxi with my own money. Within a few months, I joined the fleet. I remember my first trip from Lower Parel to Worli Naka—it was 6 a.m. when two ladies sat in my taxi. They'd never seen a female taxi driver before and were so impressed!

But some men in the union did everything to make things tough. Fifteen days in, I was struggling to make a U-turn; so one of them asked, 'If you can't even get the basics right, how will you ever drive?' But one of the other drivers encouraged me to prove them wrong! Once, an elderly gentleman said, 'Back in my village I've heard that women are making progress in cities, but this is the first time I've witnessed it.' I was so overwhelmed. It's been three years since then and driving this taxi has put me in the driver's seat of my life. Once my husband and I were discussing the roles of men and women, when I told him that, 'A woman can do everything that a man can.' We placed a bet to see who would win—looks like I did!

I GREW UP IN THE MIDDLE EAST and recently moved to Kerala for my undergrad. Growing up, I always wore a Hijab. But, a while ago, I decided to not wear it. At first, all hell broke loose!

My freedom was seen as 'rebellious'. Relatives would call my parents and complain about it. And the complaints slowly became 'threats'.

Eventually, all the relatives decided that because I wasn't wearing a Hijab, not only me but my cousins too wouldn't find boys. I was suddenly the reason behind my cousin sister not getting married! My one decision, lead to things I never imagined. My every move was now being questioned—even my job! I was scared that my education too would come to a halt. But I never gave up. Initially, my father did question my choice, but when he understood that it was 'my choice', he became my pillar. My mother too! For me, that was the biggest gift—my parents supporting me during a time when others wouldn't. I've always felt that wearing a hijab is an individual prerogative. I wore it for years before realising that I had a choice. And when I knew I had one, I took a decision that I felt was right for me. To the ones who wear it, you have my utmost respect. To the ones who choose not to, don't let anyone tell you otherwise.

TRIGGER WARNING attempted suicide: My dad remarried because he felt he deserved better than his first wife. When he brought his second wife home, she was shattered. I was born to my dad's new wife a year later. But my dad's first wife felt more like a mom to me than my own—I call her Aai. Mom would drop me to Aai's house when she went to work.

Aai loved cooking for me and talking to me. Sometimes it felt like she loved me more than her own kids. But when mom saw how close we were getting, she tried keeping Aai away. In fact, she beat me if she saw me with anyone. Once, when I was with a friend, she told her parents, 'Your daughter is not as educated as mine. Keep her out of my sight.'

I was devastated—at fifteen, I was left with no friends. In a fit of rage, I jumped off my balcony. While falling, I could only think of Aai. Luckily, I only fractured a leg. Over time, mom apologised. But her niceness was short lived—she still yells at me if I'm ever with friends or Aai. I do it anyway. I still spend a lot of time with Aai—I'm happiest around her. My mom may be my biological mother, but if anyone's treated me like a daughter, it's Aai ... and Aai is mom.

AS A CHILD I WAS NEVER GOOD at academics—I'd bounce between C's and E's and was constantly bullied for it. So, I focused on sports. But during a game, I suffered a knee injury. While recovering, my doctor advised me to cycle regularly. I fell in love with the outdoors. Over time, I got fascinated with the idea of long-distance cycle touring. After my 10th exams, I decided to cycle from Kashmir to Kanyakumari. I sold my mobile, borrowed from friends, and took Rs 1500 from mom. It took twenty-four days. I was just sixteen; throughout my journey, I wept, I screamed and slept on footpaths. I even got mugged.

But it was an experience of a lifetime. When I finally returned home, I realised that I learnt more during those twenty-four days than I had in my twleve years of schooling. So after 12th, while my friends were preparing for their careers, I had no goal—I toured South-East Asia on my bicycle. For a whole year, I travelled through ten countries. Sadly I had to cut my journey short when I got injured in Vietnam. I came back home and had all the time in the world to think about my next step—that's when I decided to opt out of a formal education. To sustain, I did odd jobs—I wrote, shot photographs, edited videos, chopped vegetables and sold sports equipment.

I had clarity for the first time—I wanted a simple life where I had enough to eat and meet new people every day. Initially, my parents weren't supportive. It took time, but once they saw that I was taking care of myself, they came around. I even managed to save a good amount and I moved to the Himalayas. So here I am today, unlearning, creating, bonding, but most importantly ... living. I know that I'll never have that fancy house, fancy car or any of those material things, but I'm free and I have happiness; isn't that what this is all about?

FOUR DAYS AFTER HE WAS BORN, Neel stopped taking my feed; he'd sleep all day. I rushed him to the hospital. The doctors put him under observation for twenty-four hours. Those twenty-four hours turned into eleven days; Neel was diagnosed with a condition that leads to organ failure. Phrases like, 'stunted growth', 'short life span' and 'special child' were thrown at me.

I couldn't believe my little boy, who had just opened his eyes to the world, was already in so much pain. When his treatment began, I wanted to spend every waking moment with him because I didn't know how much time he had. I still don't ... On day five, Neel was put on a ventilator. I held his tiny hand and whispered, 'I understand your pain, it's okay if you want to let go.'

But he fought hard and a month later we took him home. Honestly, bringing up a child with this condition takes a toll on you—financially and emotionally. His food has to be shipped from the US. I have to be extra careful about infections; It gets overwhelming, but when I see Neel in his element, nothing else matters. He loves being outdoors, and if you raise your voice at him, he will 'hup' you. Of course, I still have my off days; a couple of days ago a twelve year old girl with a similar condition passed away ... When I heard the news, I sank. I spent the entire day crying, until Neel said one word, 'Happy!' Neel turned twenty-one months old today.

He's taught me so much about valuing every moment; of not giving up. Every birthday celebrated is a milestone, each day gone by is an achievement. But while we worry about the small things, he's busy loving life. He's always so happy; you will never see him cry. Just look!

TRIGGER WARNING I was born with a disability—my face was different, and I didn't have an ear. My mother cried when the doctors told her about my condition. Growing up in Patna, I always knew I was different. Eventually my mother became my biggest support. She'd tell me to reach for the stars and explore anything I had an interest in. But in the outside world, it wasn't as easy. I'd never be looked at the way an average pretty girl would be looked at. Even relatives would come up with all sorts of 'advice' on how I can become better.

Even my own grandmother didn't try to hide how much she didn't like me. Every year at Christmas all the kids would get amazing gifts from her, but I'd get the cheapest, most convenient thing. I remember once my aunt said, 'You know your grandmother hates you right?' That was one of the most heart-breaking moments of my life. I'd spend my days studying and working, but I'd cry myself to to sleep every night. Around that time, I moved with my parents to Delhi—I joined a college and finally started to feel at peace. But that's when the whole idea of me getting a surgery to 'fix' my ear was spoken about on a daily basis. I'd be encouraged at home to go for it because no one would marry me otherwise. I couldn't understand why it was such a big deal. Eventually, a cousin advised me not to do it—she told me I wasn't lacking in any way. That's when I called the idea off. Since then, it's always felt like it was just me against the whole world. And when my then boyfriend cheated on me, it was too much for me to deal with. So I took a lot of sleeping pills. Somehow, nothing happened and I went to work the next day as if everything was normal. But it wasn't—I was at rock bottom.

I needed to stop feeling like a charity case I forced myself to heal—I started writing and over time I realized I couldn't let my self-worth depend on anyone else but me. This last year, I've felt more like myself than ever before. I'm learning to look in the mirror, day after day, and love what I see.

I STARTED WRITING AND OVER TIME I REALIZED I COULDN'T LET MY SELF-WORTH DEPEND ON ANYONE ELSE BUT ME.

Levi's

I HAD MY FIRST PANIC ATTACK when I was nineteen. It started when a teacher in my second year of engineering began bullying me. Once I even copied an assignment that got full marks, and he still failed me! It got so bad that one day, I threw up right outside the college gate. I ran from there, and just sat at a beach for five hours. That soon became a pattern. My heart would pound just at the thought of going to college. But I didn't have the courage to tell my parents I wanted to quit! I just waited until the day the college asked me to leave because of low attendance, and then told my parents. At first, they were upset. I come from an academic family, and it was shameful for them to say that their son had quit. We would barely talk—so I took up an internship just to get out of the house. Eventually, we found our way back to each other—they weren't upset because I dropped out; it was because of how I did it. My mom knew engineering didn't make me happy, so at her suggestion, I joined a media course. There, I was in a healthy environment, but there were days when I'd chew the insides of my mouth to shreds because I couldn't control my restlessness. The worst was when I would lash out at my loved ones ... I began working as a stand-up comedian, so I spent a lot of time on social media, and it can be a very toxic place. Simple comments like, 'You're not funny, quit!' would kick start a tornado of thoughts. My anxiety would make me feel like everything I was doing was pointless. I hit rock bottom after the AIB roast debacle. Imagine waking up to newspapers and channels calling you a stain on the face of the nation! I felt helpless when the cops showed up at my mom's door. I didn't know how to face people, so I'd just be cooped up at a friend's place for days on end. I was in a very dark place. But my family and friends never gave up on me. Even today, I wake up to simple messages like, 'Hey, just a feelings check!' I went for therapy, took up regular exercise, and disconnected from things that triggered my anxiety.

MY HEART WOULD POUND JUST AT THE THOUGHT OF GOING TO COLLEGE.

But I still have bad days. No matter how much I tell myself to not get affected by a random person's words, it happens. But I'm learning to deal. My journey of selfhealing is an ongoing battle, and I'm okay with that. Because I've realized that I don't have to go at it alone. I don't have to give in, or give up. I just have to keep fighting.

I GOT MARRIED DURING A TIME when taking a honeymoon trip wasn't even in the rule book. The maximum distance we would go to was our village near the city. Now, years have passed since then. My kids are settled, so are their kids, and their kids' kids. Finally, after all this time, my journey has begun once again. I have a group of friends with whom I go on trips. We contribute money through the year and then organise full fledged vacation for us all. It might not look like it, but I've visited tons of places in India—from Kanyakumari to Kerala, from Bangalore to Goa. I'm a very experienced traveller now! I'm already planning my next trip to Delhi, and after that I want to see the Taj Mahal. I began traveling when I was seventy, and I don't see myself stopping anytime soon. Age is just a number at the end of the day.

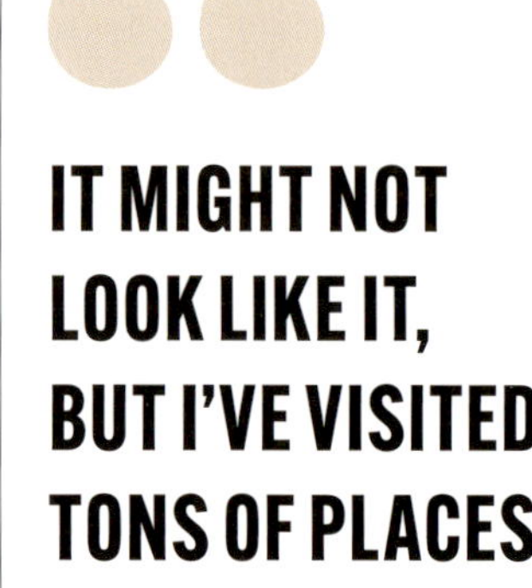

IT MIGHT NOT LOOK LIKE IT, BUT I'VE VISITED TONS OF PLACES IN INDIA.

OUR SHOPS ARE RIGHT NEXT TO EACH OTHER—we've been working here together for fifty-five years now. We open our shops every morning and then sit together for the rest of the day. Every day, we talk about our work, or our families. We don't need to have something specific to talk about. Sometimes he comes with me to the mandir, or I go with him to the mosque. At the end of the day, we go home together—we're neighbours, so both our families have become one big family. I'm sixty-nine and content! Life has been kind to me, I have a wife, kids, grandkids ... even my grandkids have kids, but most importantly I've had a good friend by my side. These are the only things that matter. None of the other stuff they tell you about.

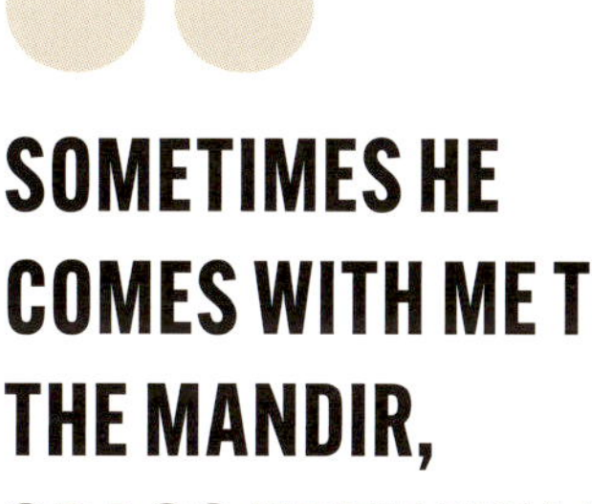

SOMETIMES HE COMES WITH ME TO THE MANDIR, OR I GO WITH HIM TO THE MOSQUE.

TEN YEARS AGO, I'd lost the will to live. My son passed away suddenly, and it was something I couldn't come to terms with. No matter how hard I tried, I couldn't move on. And it took my entire family's support to get me to where I am today. My wife is my strength, and my daughter, my happiness. My daughter's family lives with us too—I love helping my grandchildren with their homework. It makes me feel closer to my son and reminds me of the days when I used to teach him. In a way, it gives me peace. I've been a tailor for thirty years—every now and then, I see little kids come in here with their parents, and I miss my son terribly. But when I go back home every day, I get to sit down with my family for a meal, and I realise how much I have; I'm lucky to have that meal, to have my family ... to be alive.

I REALISE HOW MUCH I HAVE; I'M LUCKY TO HAVE THAT MEAL, TO HAVE MY FAMILY ... TO BE ALIVE.

I USED TO BE A HOUSEWIFE. My husband earned a meagre salary as a railway coolie; most of which was spent by him on alcohol. Whatever was left was never enough for me and our three children. Every day he would come home drunk, and beat me. I would clench my teeth and bear it—I had no one to complain to. I don't know how right it is to say this, but perhaps God understood my plight, and took my husband away a few years ago.

But I wasn't educated, and had to fend for my kids—I had no idea what to do. But to my surprise, a few days after his death, my husband's job was offered to me. I was sceptical at first because I had never seen a woman coolie; I would be the only female amongst fifty males! How would I manage? But what choice did I also have? I had to do what was right for my kids and their future—I made up my mind and took the job.

Turns out, I had nothing to worry about—the men have been really kind and encouraging; like family. People often hesitate to ask me to carry their luggage, and are amused that I'm a woman coolie. But I just smile and carry on with my work. And whenever I have stressful thoughts, I've learnt to drop it and take a break when it gets too heavy, just like my customers' baggage!

SEEN IN VAPI

WHEN I WAS TWELVE, my family moved to Srinagar where bloodshed was the norm. I hated violence. One day, I convinced my classmates to protest—we made white flags and walked the streets. Unexpectedly, firing started; a known shopkeeper rescued me. Abbu kept a strict eye on me after that. But my aunt convinced Ammi to put me in a Madrasa. On the first day itself, I saw how patriarchal the teachers were—any girl who questioned their teachings was beaten up. Infuriated, I screamed, 'Yaha mujhe Khuda nazar nahi aate'. I was locked up in a room for months. I fell severely ill—the Maulanas had to take me to the hospital. When Abbu saw me, he was shocked—I had boils all over; he took me home at once. But Ammi still blamed me. Abbu would travel for work—once when he was away my brother sent me back to the Madrasa. I was eighteen when I ran away, first to Delhi and then to Mumbai. With my savings I enrolled in a computer course. Whilst in Mumbai, a photographer spotted me and asked me to try modelling. Within a short span, I made a name for myself. All was well until my photo was misused for a kamasutra ad. Abbu, sent the cops to look for me. I was forced to go back to Kashmir. Three years later, I ran away to Bombay again. I restarted my career—I was featured in magazines like Vogue and Grazia. It's been ten years since I came to Bombay; I want to buy my own house and settle here. All my life I've been on the run—from my parents, from patriarchy. But if that's what it takes to live my life on my own terms, so be it.

MY DAD USED TO BE A BANKER and was transferred frequently. By the time I completed my B.Sc, I had studied in thirteen different institutions. Being exposed to a variety of places had a great influence on me. Once I graduated, I got into the real estate business. But fitness has always been a passion of mine. One day, when I was forty-eight, one of my gym friends proposed that we run the 21K Midnight Marathon. The idea seemed ridiculous. But we decided to try anyway, just for kicks. On the day, I was exhausted by the 10.5 Km mark. I was ready to call it quits, when I heard a distinct voice from the crowd. 'Go daddy!' It was the oldest of my three daughters. I couldn't bear to let her down. I somehow pushed myself to complete the race. That was it, and I was hooked. Today, I organize triathlons and have even founded a runners club in Mysore. As a kid, I was always fascinated with the idea of growing my own food. It was this dream that got me to shift base; I now live in a one acre piece of land.

There's more money to be made in the city, but here, I have dogs and rabbits for company I have my precious plants to keep me occupied, and my lovely wife to share the home with. Going to the lake for a swim, or the hill nearby for a run, now that's what I call life!

MY CHILDHOOD DAYS were the happiest. We lived in a small town near Nashik where life was very peaceful. There was a river near our house where all of us kids would splash about—sometimes we even took our buffaloes! After marriage, my husband and I moved to Bombay and pretty soon I realised that city life wasn't as easy. He used to work as a driver and earned Rs 100 a month, so to make ends meet we shared one small room with three other families. I took up some sewing work as well to help us raise our children better. Finally, after saving for years, we were able to move to a house on rent. Small and cozy, it was home. As life became better and our kids started earning, I realised looking back, that even though it wasn't always rosy—those were the days. The times when we would share bhelpuri on special occasions, or when he would request his boss if he could take me for a spin in their car after work hours. Our weekends spent at Mahalaxmi temple, or the time we would all huddle together during the Bombay monsoons and share cups of tea.

I'm old now, my husband is long gone and my grandchildren are chasing their dreams, but the one piece of advice I can give you is to hold onto those smaller memories, those little joys that make life. Ultimately, when you reach my age, you'll know that those are the things that will make you smile ... and then you're ready to go happily!

I WAS TWELVE WHEN THE EARTHQUAKE hit us. When everything started shaking violently, my mother screamed at me to run. I managed to reach the parking lot, but that's when the entire building collapsed on me. I lost consciousness. I came back to my senses a few hours later—it was really dark. My right hand was caught in the window of a crushed car—I vividly remember the pain and my throat being so dry, that I couldn't even shout for help. With my left hand, I managed to reach a bucket that had dirty water and drank from it.

I then tried cutting my right hand with a piece of glass, but the pain was too much I screamed for help, but no one came. I didn't know when the fire brigade arrived and attempted to remove the debris.

Finally, they dug a tunnel to get to me. They tried to save my hand, but amputation was the only option. I felt every moment of excruciating pain as the knife cut through my skin and bone. I lost consciousness again. When I woke up, I got to know that I was trapped for thirty-six hours.

My recovery after that was difficult. I only got through it because I was surrounded by amazing friends and family. Now, I've learned to live this new life independently; including driving a car by myself. I'm a psychiatrist and also happily married today. I can't change the past—the only thing I'm in control of is my today and tomorrow, and that's what I'm focused on. One day at a time.

FEW YEARS AGO, my teeth started protruding—I started to feel very insecure. I would cover my mouth, not only when I smiled, but also while talking. I felt ugly. It reached a point where I stopped smiling altogether. After a while, my husband confronted me and said, 'Stop hiding your face—it's perfect!' But that didn't change anything for me; I still felt very under confident. So every day, he started coming up with new ways to make me laugh! He calls me 'beautiful', 'rani' and what not. I start blushing and inevitably smile ... and then I shoo him away.

THIS IS MY BEST FRIEND, SWEETY. I love her the most in the world! Sometimes when I don't love her, she gets angry at me. But she's always cuddling with me. We love going out a lot. My papa gets really worried because I keep forgetting my name.

He's written it on my forehead, so if I get lost and somebody asks me, I can just point here. But I'm not scared, as long as I have Sweety with me, I'll always find my way back home!

WE LOVE GOING OUT A LOT—MY PAPA GETS REALLY WORRIED BECAUSE I KEEP FORGETTING MY NAME.

ACKNOWLEDGEMENTS

It always takes a village.

My parents and sisters, Prerna and Chandni, my brothers-in-law Karan and Chintan—thank you for putting up with my endless rants and the plummeting lows of work and life of a woman consumed in business—there is no 'me' without you.

My best friends—Anuja, Shreya, Tiffany, Divya, Yash, Vaidya, Chesta, Sakshi, Poonam, Jiten, Aadi, Harshil, Keshav, Veena, Masoom—thank you for accompanying me on this journey and being the best friends a girl could wish for.

The team at Humans of Bombay—every writer and photographer who has allowed this dream to become a reality and everyone at the HOB HQ who has been working tirelessly on the book launch, but most importantly to Devanshi, who's not only built this book, but Humans of Bombay with me—this is our baby! And Kirtishree, for joining in and providing a semblance of method to our madness! Also, Unnati, for being a pain in my bum (just kidding!); for managing my otherwise unmanageable and chaotic life.

The team at HarperCollins India—Swati, Bonita and Twisha—for accommodating our every request and making our vision, yours.

And finally, to every person who opened their hearts and poured into the ink of our virtual pens—thank you for being the best humans in the world.